LONDON COMMUTER LINES

Volume 1

• SILVER LINK TRAVELLING COMPANION •

LONDON COMMUTER LINES

A history of the capital's suburban railways in the BR era 1948-95

Volume 1: Main lines north of the Thames

Frank Hornby

• RAILWAY HERITAGE •
from
The NOSTALGIA Collection

First published by Silver Link Publishing Ltd in one volume as *London Suburban* in August 1995
First published in paperback in two volumes in 1999
Reprinted 2002

British Library Cataloguing in Publication Data

A catalogue record for this book is available from the British Library.

ISBN 1 85794 115 2

Silver Link Publishing Ltd
The Trundle
Ringstead Road
Great Addington
Kettering
Northants NN14 4BW

Tel/Fax: 01536 330588
email: sales@nostalgiacollection.com
Website: www.nostalgiacollection.com

Printed and bound in Great Britain

A Silver Link book
from
The NOSTALGIA *Collection*

ACKNOWLEDGEMENTS

My grateful thanks are due to Mr N. L. Browne for his many helpful comments and suggestions; also to those who have kindly contributed photographs from their collections, as credited.

BIBLIOGRAPHY

In compiling this work, in addition to numerous maps and timetables, the following sources of information have proved invaluable:

BR Diary 1979-1985, J. Glover
British Electric Trains, H. Linecar
British Rail Motive Power (Ian Allan)
LCGB Bulletin 1979-1994
London and its Railways, R. Davies and M. D. Grant
London's Railway History, H. P. White
London's Termini, Alan A. Jackson
'London Suburban Railway' Series, V. Mitchell and K. Smith (Middleton Press)
Motive Power Recognition – DMUs and EMUs, C. J. Marsden
Modern Railways 1962-1964
Railway Magazine 1931-1994
Railway Observer 1948-1994
RCTS Locomotive Histories, LBSC, LSWR, SECR
Railways of South East England
Railway World 1961-1985
Regional History of Railways – Southern England, H. P. White
Register of Closed Stations, C. R. Clinker
Southern Electric 1909-79, G. T. Moody
The Great Eastern Railway, C. J. Allen
The North London Railway, M. Robbins
The South Eastern & Chatham Railway, O. S. Nock
The South Western Railway, C. H. Ellis
Trains Illustrated 1954-1964

CONTENTS

London suburban steam locomotive types

Class	Type	Designer	Introduced (year)	Cylinders (No) (in x in)	Boiler pressure (lb/sq in)	Driving wheels (ft-in)	Weight (tons-cwt)	Tractive effort (lb)
Western Region								
61XX	2-6-2T	Collett	1931	(2) 18 x 30	225	5-8	78-9	27340
54XX	0-6-0PT	Collett	1931	(2) 16½ x 24	165	5-2	46-12	14780
14XX	0-4-2T	Collett	1932	(2) 16 x 24	165	5-2	41-6	13895
London Midland Region								
4P	2-6-4T	Fowler	1928	(2) 19 x 26	200	5-9	86-5	23125
4P	2-6-4T	Stanier	1934	(3) 16 x 26	200	5-9	92-5	24600
4P	2-6-4T	Stanier	1935	(2) 19⅜ x 26	200	5-9	87-17	24670
4P	2-6-4T	Fairburn	1945	(2) 19⅜ x 26	200	5-9	85-5	24670
3P	2-6-2T	Fowler	1930	(2) 17½ x 26	200	5-3	71-16	21486
3P	2-6-2T	Stanier	1935	(2) 17½ x 26	200	5-3	71-5	21486
2P	2-6-2T	Ivatt	1946	(2) 16 x 24	200	5-0	63-5	17400
2P	0-4-4T	Stanier	1932	(2) 18 x 26	160	5-7	58-1	17099
3P	4-4-2T	Whitelegg	1923	(2) 19 x 26	170	6-6	71-10	17390
Eastern Region								
A5	4-6-2T	Robinson	1911	(2) 20 x 26	180	5-7	85-18	23743
L1	2-6-4T	Thompson	1945	(2) 20 x 26	225	5-2	89-9	32080
C14	4-4-2T	Robinson	1907	(2) 18 x 26	160	5-7	71-0	17100
N1	0-6-2T	Ivatt	1907	(2) 18 x 26	170	5-8	65-17	17900
N2	0-6-2T	Gresley	1920	(2) 19 x 26	170	5-8	71-9	19945
N5	0-6-2T	Parker	1889	(2) 18 x 26	160	5-1	62-12	18781
N7	0-6-2T	Hill	1915	(2) 18 x 24	180	4-10	64-17	20512
F5	2-4-2T	Holden	1903	(2) 17½ x 24	180	5-4	56-8	17571
British Railways Standard								
4P	2-6-4T	Riddles	1952	(2) 18 x 28	225	5-8	86-13	25100

INTRODUCTION

When the first passenger railways opened for business in London in the 1830s, the capital's population was around 1¾ million, concentrated into an area of some 20 square miles. Most people still lived within walking distance of their workplaces, while those wealthy enough to reside in the villas in outlying districts enjoyed the convenience of their own carriages.

Not surprisingly therefore the first trunk lines gave little thought to short-distance passengers, and indeed the termini in Euston Square and Paddington were then quite close to the fringes of the built-up areas. At first, on the London & Birmingham line, there was only Harrow station south of Watford, with just five trains calling in each direction daily, while on the Great Western there was only West Drayton between Paddington and Slough, albeit joined shortly afterwards by Ealing, Hanwell and Southall.

However, there soon followed, just north of the Thames, one line of a very different character. The London & Blackwall, opened in July 1840 and initially cable-worked, was only 3½ miles long and served a densely populated area as a harbinger of the many commuter lines to come. Thereafter the relentless population growth, causing the city's boundaries to move ever outwards, was accompanied by a steady expansion of the suburban network, most of which was in place by the end of the 1870s. By far the greatest concentration of new routes was to the north and north-east, out of King's Cross, Liverpool Street, Fenchurch Street and Broad Street, and with the exception of the latter all this traffic remained steam-worked for many years, until after nationalisation. Even the Great Eastern, with its intensive 'Jazz' services, spurned electrification, and indeed in 1902 had experimented with a monster but short-lived 'high-acceleration' 0-10-0 tank engine.

On the main lines north of the river electric traction was confined to the LNWR, on which it was adopted for the services out of Euston and Broad Street to Watford and Richmond, in stages between 1914 and 1922.

Prominent in the network were jointly operated lines such as the North & South Western Junction, Tottenham & Hampstead Junction, West London, and Metropolitan Widened Lines, over which there was a variety of cross-London services, some of which were short-lived, succumbing to competition from rival forms of transport or to cut-backs during the First World War.

Concurrently with the expansion of surface lines there was similar activity below ground, commencing with the first sections of the Metropolitan and District Railways. Later these two companies extended their routes, still steam-worked, to the north and west into almost virgin countryside, stimulating a rash of housing development. Meantime, deep 'tube' lines were under construction, built to a smaller loading gauge and multiplied during the Edwardian era, eventually 'coming up for air' in the suburbs, with Bakerloo Line trains sharing tracks with the LNWR between Queens Park and Watford from 1917. Later, in the 1940s, extensions of the Northern Line replaced LNER services to High Barnet and Mill Hill East, with the Central Line following suit to Hainault and Epping in the east and to West Ruislip in the west. The formation of the London Passenger Transport Board in 1933 had brought surface and underground lines into one administration with buses, trams and trolleybuses, resulting in a public service second to none in the world.

Under the stewardship of British Railways from 1948 to the onset of privatisation, steam traction was eliminated, as was vintage stock such as the LNER articulated sets, replaced eventually on most routes by electric multiple units, and accompanied by the virtual disappearance of semaphore signals and their replacement by colour lights controlled from a few 'signalling centres'.

Generally during these years services improved both in speed and frequency, although with London's population dwindling, many commuters now travel to and fro over much longer distances. Doubtless expedited by the formation of 'Network SouthEast' in the 1980s, north-south services saw something of a revival, with 'Thameslink' trains plying between the former Midland and Southern Regions from 1985.

Since the demise of British Rail, a number of Train Operating Companies have taken over from NSE in providing suburban services north of the Thames as follows:

Thames Trains	from Paddington
Chiltern Railway Co	from Marylebone
Thameslink Rail	between Bedford and 'South Central' destinations via Blackfriars
Silverlink Train Services	from Euston, and between Willesden and Clapham Junction, and on the North London and Tottenham & Hampstead lines
West Anglia Great Northern	from King's Cross, and from Liverpool Street via Hackney Downs
Great Eastern Railway	from Liverpool Street via Stratford
LTS Rail	from Fenchurch Street

Having set the scene, let us now look in greater detail
at how London's suburban services fared
between 1948 and 1995.

1.
LINES FROM PADDINGTON

Paddington-Reading
West Ealing-Greenford
West Drayton-Staines West and Uxbridge (Vine Street)
Slough-Windsor and Slough Trading Estate
Maidenhead-Marlow and High Wycombe
Twyford-Henley-on-Thames
Old Oak Common-High Wycombe via Greenford

If there were league tables for the suburban traffic handled by the London termini, Paddington would barely scrape into the second division, let alone be in contention with the 'front runners' like Liverpool Street and Waterloo. In the early years of the Great Western Railway, with sights set firmly on Bristol and points west, scant regard was shown for the modest communities between London and Reading – even Royal Windsor was bypassed and had to be content with a branch line from Slough – and the 1839 timetable listed just four 'short trains' daily, between Paddington and West Drayton. In more recent times the popular GWR image was one of splendid trains hauled by locomotives with regal (or saintly) names, and to the lineside spotter the 'locals' behind their less glamorous tank engines were scarcely worth a glance!

By the 1930s ribbon development along the arterial roads west of London had attracted concentrations of industry to locations such as Southall, Hayes and Slough, so that while this brought short-distance custom to the railway, much of it was between these and other intermediate stations. Moreover, interchange with the District and Central Lines at Ealing Broadway siphoned many passengers away from Paddington. Nevertheless, as the towns along the line grew steadily, so did the traffic, requiring progressively heavier and more frequent trains.

By 1951 suburban traffic was up by 25 per cent as compared with pre-war years, and although adversely affected by the motoring boom in the 1960s, revived again, notably with a further 25 per cent increase in the five years from 1986. By then the population of Slough had topped the 100,000 mark, with Reading approaching double that figure and Maidenhead reaching 60,000 – a far cry from the small towns and villages along Brunel's 'Great Way to the West'!

Routes and infrastructure

The 36 miles of main line between Paddington and Reading have been four-tracked since 1893, soon after the abolition of the broad gauge, providing a separate pair for stopping passenger and goods trains. With easy gradients – no steeper than 1 in 1200 – and with only 15 intermediate stations, a reasonably smartly timed service is possible.

At Paddington the suburban station has none of the grandeur of its main-line counterpart, to which it is linked only by a footbridge. It formed a separate entity known as Bishop's Road until it was rebuilt and enlarged in 1933, since when it has consisted of two 600-foot island platforms with faces numbered 13-16, originally serving four through tracks, the inner pair for the GWR and the outer for the Metropolitan's Hammersmith & City line trains, allowing cross-platform interchange. After extensive alterations, completed in November 1967, the tracks at platforms 13 and 14 became terminal roads for Western Region use, while those at Nos 15 and 16 remained through lines for the Hammersmith & City service. Some outer suburban trains operate from platforms in the main station, usually Nos 11 or 12.

The 1967 reorganisation provided separate tracks for the Metropolitan, passing through Royal Oak station a mere quarter of a mile away before burrowing beneath the BR running lines at Subway Junction to emerge at Westbourne Park. A long footbridge linked the Metropolitan and BR stations here until the latter, 1¼ miles from Paddington, closed in March 1992.

At Old Oak Common Junction the erstwhile direct line to Birmingham diverges from the Reading main line, which continues due west through Acton and Ealing Broadway, a busy

PADDINGTON, MARYLEBONE AND BAKER STREET

Ex-GWR
Ex-GCR
Ex-GWR/GCR Joint line
Ex-Metropolitan Railway
Ex-Met/GCR Joint line

The next station is West Ealing, beyond which the Greenford loop branches off in a northerly direction to join up the two main lines, serving three intermediate halts in 2 miles before terminating in a bay platform at Greenford (Central Line) station. The loop, double track throughout, opened in 1903 and is mostly on embankments, with a 320-foot viaduct over the River Brent and a girder bridge across Western Avenue. At South Greenford the southbound platform was temporarily demolished in 1993 so that intending passengers for the Ealing direction had first to go northwards to Greenford and return from there! Triangular junctions at both ends make the loop a useful diversionary route when required.

Back on the main line, Hanwell station still retains much of its 'GWR' atmosphere, with original buildings and modern lighting in the shape of old gas lamps! After crossing Wharncliffe Viaduct we reach Southall, 9 miles from Paddington, where the one-time locomotive depot of post-war construction still stands, on the south side of the line in the 'vee' of the junction with the Brentford branch. The latter lost its passenger service in 1942, and proposals for its reopening in 1954 did not come to fruition.

Two stations further on, West Drayton was until the 1960s the junction for two branches, one south to Staines West – still partly open for freight traffic – and the other north to Uxbridge (Vine Street). Trains for both branches were accommodated at the outer face of the up island platform, and they shared a common exit from the west end before the Staines branch swung away to dive under the main line and continue south for 6¼ miles.

Opened throughout in 1885 with single standard-gauge track, the passenger service to Staines lasted for 80 years. There was one intermediate station with a passing loop at Colnbrook, then three 'halts' of which the request stop at Yeoveney, with a platform just 20 feet long, was surely the smallest to feature in our 'London Suburban' survey. A wartime spur, removed in 1959, connected with the Southern Region's Staines-Windsor branch, which passes close to the Staines West

interchange station where the District and Central Lines have terminal platforms. Ealing Broadway was extensively modernised in 1965 with shops and kiosks sharing the entrance hall with the booking office. More recently this and other stations have had their platforms resurfaced and lengthened in preparation for the 'Network Turbos'.

Suburban lines from Paddington, main line and branches

Miles	Name	Opened	Closed	Notes
From Paddington				
0	Paddington	6/1838		Present station opened 1854
1¼	Westbourne Park	10/1871	3/1992	
4¼	Acton main line	2/1868		
5¾	Ealing Broadway	12/1838		
6½	West Ealing	3/1871		'Castle Hill Ealing' to 1899
7¼	Hanwell & Elthorne	12/1838		
9	Southall	5/1839		
10¾	Hayes & Harlington	5/1864		
13¼	West Drayton	6/1838		'West Drayton & Yiewsley' to 5/1974
14¾	Iver	12/1924		
16¼	Langley	1845		
18½	Slough	6/1838		
21	Burnham	1899		'Burnham Beeches' to 9/1930; 'Burnham (Bucks)' to 5/1975
22½	Taplow	6/1838		Originally 'Maidenhead'
24¼	Maidenhead	7/1839		Original station closed 1871
31	Twyford	7/1839		
36	Reading	3/1844		'Reading General' to 5/1973
Paddington to High Wycombe				
9¼	Greenford	1904		
10¼	Northolt	5/1907	11/1948	
11¾	South Ruislip	1908		
12¼	Ruislip Gardens	7/1934	7/1958	
13½	West Ruislip for Ickenham	1906		
16¼	Denham for Harefield	4/1906		GW&GC Joint
17¼	Denham Golf Club Platform	1912		
19	Gerrards Cross	1906		
21¼	Seer Green	1915		
23¼	Beaconsfield for Penn	1906		
28	High Wycombe	1854		
Greenford loop				
	West Ealing			
½	Drayton Green	3/1905		
1	Castle Bar Park	5/1904		
1¾	South Greenford	9/1926		
2¾	Greenford	10/1904		
Uxbridge branch				
	West Drayton			
1½	Cowley	10/1904	9/1962	
2½	Uxbridge (Vine St)	9/1856	9/1962	'Uxbridge' to 5/1907

Miles	Name	Opened	Closed	Notes
Staines West branch				
	West Drayton			
2½	Colnbrook Estate Halt	5/1961	3/1965	
3	Colnbrook	8/1884	3/1965	
3¼	Poyle Estate Halt	1/1954	3/1965	
3¾	Poyle Halt for Stanwell Moor	6/1927	3/1965	
5¼	Yeoveney	3/1892	3/1965	'Runemede Range' to 1935
6¼	Staines West	11/1885	3/1965	
Windsor branch				
	Slough			
2¾	Windsor & Eton Central	10/1849		'Windsor & Eton' to 1/1950
Henley-on-Thames branch				
	Twyford			
1¾	Wargrave	1900		
2¾	Shiplake	6/1857		
4½	Henley-on-Thames	6/1857		
Bourne End, Marlow and High Wycombe branches				
	Maidenhead			
1¼	Furze Platt Halt	7/1937		
3	Cookham	8/1854		
4½	Bourne End	8/1854		'Marlow Road' to 1874
2¼	Marlow	6/1873		
5¾	Wooburn Green	8/1854	5/1970	
7¼	Loudwater	8/1854	5/1970	
(9	High Wycombe)			
From Slough				
1½	Slough Trading Estate	1919	1/1956	

terminus. The station building here began its existence as a mill manager's house, conveniently situated for conversion when the railway arrived!

By contrast, the Uxbridge (Vine Street) branch, opened in 1856 and converted from the broad gauge in 1871, was doubled in 1880, being much the busier of the two. The only intermediate station in its 2½-mile length was at Cowley, and the terminus consisted of an island platform with adjacent goods yard. Passenger services ceased on 8 September 1962, though freight traffic continued until July 1964.

Another 9½ miles and five stations to the west is Slough, with four through platforms, an east-facing bay on the up side for terminating trains, and another on the down side at the west end for the Windsor branch. The station is a well-preserved example of classical red-bricked GWR architecture. Until closure in June 1964 a five-road locomotive shed occupied a site adjacent to a triangular junction giving access to the branch from both directions. Later, diesel multiple units were stabled on sidings inside the triangle; the western arm, once used by excursions from far and near, has since been removed.

The 2¾-mile Windsor branch opened in 1849 with no stations en route (a short-lived one opened at Chalvey in 1929) and was double

Drayton Green is one of the three 'halts' on the Greenford Loop, and is near the triangle junction with the main line at West Ealing. In this view, *circa* 1953, Collett 0-4-2T No 1446, in pristine condition, is in charge of an auto-saloon on a Greenford service. Note the junction in the background, the corrugated iron shelter, and the gas lighting. *Lens of Sutton*

Prominently displaying reporting number '2A82', railcar W55023 of Pressed Steel construction awaits departure from Staines West on 26 April 1963. The station building pre-dated the railway and was adapted from commercial use. Note the London Transport double-decker parked outside – a welcome example of road-rail co-operation. *J. M. Tolson*

track until singled in 1963. Windsor & Eton Central terminus was an altogether superior affair, approached on brick arches with a 200-foot bowstring girder bridge across the Thames. The station was rebuilt in 1897, very much with Royal travellers in mind, boasting five platform faces, a Royal waiting room, and an arched roof, a la Paddington in miniature, over the entrance. Although now reduced to one platform, at least it is still open, with a more frequent service than it enjoyed in its prime, though such events as 'Jubilee'-hauled excursions arriving via Slough West curve are but distant memories. In recent years part of the station was incorporated into a museum, complete with 'Royal Train' and waxwork passengers and staff!

Mention should also be made of another short and less well known branch from Slough to the Trading Estate 1½ miles to the west. Before closure in January 1956 it had an island platform at the terminus for its unadvertised passenger service.

Continuing down the main line through Burnham (Bucks) and Taplow, the Thames is crossed by Brunel's famous arched bridge, widened when the relief lines were laid. At Maidenhead station, some way beyond the river, there is cross-platform connection on the 'up' side with trains for the branch north to Bourne End – now a two-track terminus where reversal is necessary for those continuing along the further short branch to Marlow.

The line was opened from Maidenhead through to High Wycombe as the independent Wycombe Railway in August 1854, worked from the outset by the Great Western Railway, which absorbed it in February 1867. It was

Windsor station in its heyday had the look of a lesser Paddington, with a splendid glass-roofed edifice and well-protected platforms. The Swindon 'Cross Country' DMU is on an enthusiasts' rail tour, while a Pressed Steel three-car unit on the Slough shuttle service can be seen in the left background. *F. Hornby*

Only the Great Western and its Western Region successor could offer such an evocative scene within the 'London Suburban' area! Class '14XX' 0-4-2T No 1448 has arrived at Marlow from Bourne End on 17 November 1951 in charge of an auto-saloon, the ensemble being known locally as the 'Marlow Donkey'. *A. J. Pike*

converted to standard gauge in 1870. There is a halt at Furze Platt and a station at Cookham, followed by a bridge across the Thames at Bourne End where, in its through station days, there was an impressive track layout and an array of lower quadrant signals.

The Marlow branch parts company with the Maidenhead line at the platform ends and closely follows the river for 2¾ miles before terminating at a single platform, short of the site of the original station. This had been the epitome of the branch-line terminus so beloved by modellers, with a small locomotive shed, closed in 1961. The branch train, affectionately known locally as the 'Marlow Donkey', is recorded for posterity (with artist's licence!) on the inn sign of a nearby hostelry.

Before closure in May 1970 the 5½-mile continuation northward from Bourne End passed through two stations, with single platforms and sidings, at Wooburn Green and Loudwater, before climbing out of the valley of the River Wye at the approach to High Wycombe. The local service to and from Maidenhead was supplemented by through trains between Paddington and High Wycombe or Aylesbury.

Next along the main line is Twyford, 31 miles from Paddington and yet another junction, this time for a branch that curves away sharply to head north for 4½ miles to Henley-on-Thames of regatta fame. The line is in close proximity to the river, which it crosses between the two intermediate stations. Opened in June 1857, it had a chequered history, being doubled after conversion from broad to standard gauge in 1876, only to be singled again many years later in June 1961. Special trains, not shown in the public timetable, have run during the regatta week and in 1948 many

This view of Uxbridge (Vine Street) station in GWR days clearly shows the island platform, long enough for the through trains to and from Paddington, with goods sidings on the right. It closed to passenger traffic in September 1962. *Lens of Sutton*

services were designated as having 'limited accommodation', indicating the use of AEC railcars on the branch at that time. The terminus, originally with three platform faces, boasted a Brunelian roof until the old station was demolished in 1975.

Westwards from Twyford the main line passes through the steep-sided Sonning Cutting for 2 miles before emerging into open country at the approach to Reading, the outer limit for many stopping services. Some local trains terminate in a bay platform at the London end of this extremely busy station, while others are dealt with at through platforms. The depot for diesel units is on the site of the old steam shed, west of the station in the junction of the Bristol and 'Berks & Hants' main lines.

Retracing our steps to Old Oak Common Junction, the former Birmingham main line is now closely paralleled by London Underground's Central Line, opened throughout to West Ruislip in November 1948. In consequence the GWR local services were withdrawn and the stations and halts as far as Greenford closed six months prior to nationalisation. The junction with the loop line at Greenford has already been mentioned, while a flyover junction at Northolt, 2½ miles further on, marks the beginning of the line opened jointly by the GWR and GCR in 1906. This was used by express trains from both Paddington and Marylebone, so was laid out for fast running with easy gradients and loop lines at the stations for stopping trains. The through tracks have since been lifted, leaving only the platform lines in situ. The station buildings owe far more to the GWR than to the GCR, and though now served exclusively by trains from Marylebone, the neat brick buildings with wide canopies are unmistakeable in their origin.

A 2-mile branch from a junction between West Ruislip and Denham terminated in a small station at Uxbridge (High Street), opened in 1907. The meagre passenger service from Denham ceased on the outbreak of war in September 1939, though coal traffic was still handled until July 1964. A scheme to link the High Street and Vine Street stations was abandoned after some preliminary work had been started.

The line beyond Denham on to High Wycombe traverses patches of still attractive countryside and will receive further attention in the next chapter, dealing with the services out of Marylebone.

Think of typical GWR signalling and in one's mind's eye one sees lower quadrant semaphores on white posts topped with tall finials, controlled from boxes of red brick and cream-painted woodwork. But electric power signals were installed between Paddington and Southall as long ago as 1932, and new power boxes were provided at Paddington the following year. By early BR days the station approach tracks were signalled by multiple-aspect colour-lights, and the writing was on the wall for traditional methods of train control, although the transformation was gradual. Both suburban and long-distance traffic benefited from the changes, commencing in 1959 when multiple-aspect signals were installed eastwards from Acton, and authority was given to commence work on the 27 miles from Southall to Reading. A new power installation, commissioned at Slough on 13 October 1963, replaced 20 boxes controlling the main line from Hayes to Twyford and the Windsor branch, while track improvements enabled the speed limit over much of the relief lines to be raised to 75 mph. Meanwhile, on the Henley branch a computerised, electronically interlocked control system installed in 1962 was claimed to be the first of its kind in the world.

From September 1967 a new panel box at Old Oak Common took over control of the line in stages between Paddington and Hayes, linking with Slough box and, from March 1972, with Reading. A further remodelling of tracks and signalling from Paddington to West Drayton was commenced in the spring of 1992, the cost of £40 million being shared between Network SouthEast and InterCity. Preliminary work has also started on the Heathrow link, which, subject to funding, is forecast for completion in 1995/6. This involves installation of a flyover junction west of Hayes & Harlington, and eventual construction of 100 mph three-car electric units that will require only 17 minutes 'under the catenary' for the journey.

Services

The Western Region timetable for Summer 1948, in the first year of British Railways, listed 75 weekday suburban arrivals at Paddington from the Reading direction. Thirteen of these, in the early morning, were 'Workmen's', none of the 40 arrivals on Sunday being so designated. Reading was the starting point for 19, the slowest being the all-stations 09.05, allowed 103 minutes for the 36 miles, a modest 21 mph. There were of course others from beyond Reading, calling at Slough and Ealing Broadway en route and taking only half that time. Three more came from Henley-on-Thames, providing 1st Class accommodation – then denied to the strictly 'suburban' traveller –

while one was through from Marlow and five from High Wycombe. One of these gave the fastest service from Maidenhead, covering the 24¼ miles in 36 minutes, with one stop (40.4 mph).

Windsor had four through trains, one being non-stop from Slough in 26 minutes for 18 miles (41.5 mph). Of the 18 tabled as starting from Slough, two in the afternoon peak actually came from the Trading Estate branch, though not advertised as such. Eleven started from Uxbridge (Vine Street) – some pausing for a few minutes at West Drayton before continuing – and another 11 from Hayes & Harlington. There was just one up from Southall, and additionally there were a few short workings along the main line terminating at Slough, Ealing Broadway, etc, and making connections with Paddington trains. A solitary Reading to Twyford train continued thence along the branch to Henley-on-Thames after reversal.

All in all, this judicious mix of semi-fast and stopping trains ensured that most stations from Reading up to West Drayton had one or more reasonably fast services to Town during the morning peak hours.

Weekday suburban arrivals at Paddington from High Wycombe or beyond via Denham numbered 21, only five of which – four from Princes Risborough and one from High Wycombe – took the direct route through Park Royal. Journey time from High Wycombe ranged from 55 to 62 minutes for 28 miles. The remainder, inclusive of two from Princes Risborough, five from West Ruislip and nine from Northolt, were routed via the Greenford loop. Several of these made calls at the halts along the loop, thus supplementing the 16 daily trains from West Ruislip or Northolt to Ealing Broadway. After the Central Line extension opened on 21 November 1948 these latter started from Greenford, and from 4 July of the following year all stopping trains between High Wycombe and Paddington via Denham were withdrawn and the service concentrated on Marylebone.

The down services on all lines closely replicated those in the up direction, save that on Saturdays there were more trains around lunchtime and fewer in the late afternoon. The Sunday frequency was about half that on weekdays. The branches all enjoyed quite generous services, ranging from 16 daily between Bourne End and Maidenhead to 37 between Uxbridge and West Drayton – the latter, curiously, being the first to be closed in due course. All were still open on Sundays at that time.

Ten years later the 1958/59 timetable makes an interesting comparison, being the last in which steam traction was still pre-eminent. The 'Workmen's' designation for the early morning stopping trains had disappeared, but arrivals and departures at Paddington suburban and main-line stations were shown separately – all early morning and late evening trains being dealt with at the latter. Moreover, the through services to and from the branches were clearly identified.

As yet there were no significant changes in journey times or frequencies, save that from 1956 some off-peak branch and main-line stopping services had been reorganised on a 'regular interval' basis. Of the 76 weekday down semi-fast and stopping trains, eight went through to Uxbridge and two conveyed through coaches to Henley-on-Thames, as did five to Windsor, most of these being in the afternoon peak. High Wycombe was reached from Paddington via Maidenhead by six trains allowed between 79 and 102 minutes, as compared with around 55-60 minutes by those from Marylebone. The only services still routed by the direct line from Paddington via High Wycombe were two expresses to Birmingham and beyond, and a semi-fast to Banbury.

On the branches, Uxbridge (Vine Street) had suffered a fairly drastic reduction to 25 trains daily due to falling patronage, whereas Windsor had benefited by an increase to 41. An additional halt had opened at Poyle Estate on the Staines West branch, the overall journey time being increased by 2 or 3 minutes in consequence.

By the close of 1959 new diesel multiple units were appearing on some semi-fast turns, and within the next two years had taken over practically all suburban duties between London and Reading. A morning train between Maidenhead and High Wycombe was so worked from 21 November 1960, as were others on that line soon afterwards, including a round trip from Paddington, out via Maidenhead and back via Greenford. Even the 'Marlow Donkey' ceased to be steam-worked after 8 July 1962, in favour of a single railcar working through to and from Maidenhead.

Regrettably the transformation from steam to diesel traction was far from trouble-free, as the new suburban units were prone to breakdowns, requiring frequent substitutions by the dwindling fleet of '61XX' 2-6-2Ts with compartment stock. Later, in 1964, faced with mounting deficits, an attempt was made to win back lost custom with a more intensive service – publicised as the 'Western Commuteroutes' – providing a quarter-hourly peak-time frequency at most stations. The DMUs took over some longer runs from locomotive-hauled trains, a move resented by Season Ticket-holders accustomed to a higher standard of comfort. Matters eventually improved when, in 1968, some of the more 'customer friendly' Class 123 InterCity units were transferred to the London Division. The brunt of the work, however, continued to be borne by the Class 117 'High Density' units, which gave yeoman service for three decades – longer than their steam predecessors – until in turn displaced by a new generation of 'Network Turbos'.

In the interim there have been various timetable adjustments prompted by the constant pursuit of greater efficiency, or by problems arising from staff shortages. As previously mentioned, Uxbridge lost its passenger service in September 1962, followed by the Staines West branch in March 1965 and the Bourne End to High Wycombe line in May 1970. Cuts were proposed for the Windsor and Greenford services in 1963 and on the main line in the summer of 1968. A recasting of the timetable in May 1973 provided for a half-hourly stopping service between Paddington and Slough, connecting there with outer-suburban trains to and from Didcot. Windsor had its first off-season Sunday trains restored, but they were withdrawn from the Henley branch as of 1 January 1976. In that year ten weekday stopping trains were withdrawn on the main line, and through trains on the Henley, Marlow and Windsor branches also suffered cuts.

As from 4 March 1967, following the withdrawal of the Birkenhead expresses, a service of Birmingham 'semi-fast' trains via the direct line was introduced, giving High Wycombe the benefit of six 'non-stops' to and from Paddington. This was later reduced to four, and still further reduced in 1973 when all but one each way were diverted via Reading.

The 'Network Turbo' diesel units went into service early in 1992, initially on outer-suburban turns and eventually all but eliminating their predecessors (now, by a masterly piece of public relations, dubbed 'Heritage' units) by the end of the year. Initially, any advantage derived from their superior performance was partially offset by delays due to major track and signalling alterations at and near to Paddington.

If we conclude our survey by examining the timetable current at the time of writing in 1994 we find ample evidence of the changes over the years – not only in the trains themselves but also in travelling patterns. Of the 158 weekday arrivals listed in the Reading-Paddington table, no fewer than 54 have come from further down the line, including those from Westbury and the 'Turbo Expresses' from Oxford, all of which call at Slough. The remainder comprise 32 from Reading, two each from Maidenhead and Marlow, 35 from Slough, 32 from Greenford and one – the 'Regatta Express' – from Henley-on-Thames. Journey time from Reading with eight stops is 54 minutes – down by half an hour from the 1948 schedules. Naturally there is less scope for improvement on the remaining branches, on which the level of services does not differ radically from those of 45 years previously. Windsor has more trains daily (42 as against 36) and Henley rather fewer (23 as against 26), some of the latter being to and from Reading, reversing at Twyford. There are, however, significantly fewer through services between these branches and Paddington (Windsor has one down train but no corresponding one up).

Off peak the 'regular-interval' principle is firmly established, with four trains per hour from Reading in the weekday suburban timetable, one of which is a 'Turbo Express' from Oxford. Two connect at Slough with half-hourly stopping trains, omitting Acton Main Line. The latter is served by the half-hourly Greenford-Paddington trains, connecting with main-line trains at Ealing Broadway.

On the old Birmingham direct line just one service survives, in the shape of the 09.15 Paddington-Aylesbury, reaching High Wycombe in 32 minutes with one intermediate stop and returning from Aylesbury at 10.33.

Traction and trains

Among the locomotive fleet inherited by BR from the Great Western Railway in 1948 was a class of 70 '61XX' 2-6-2Ts, designed in 1931 specifically for the London suburban services. At nationalisation they were allocated to Old Oak (19), Southall (14), Slough (28), and Reading (9), with the remainder at Oxford. With 5 ft 8 in driving wheels and a boiler pressure of 225 lb per sq in they could cope with 300-ton trains at speeds in excess of 60 mph when required, and were responsible for most of the stopping and semi-fast services on both the Reading and High Wycombe lines. By 1950 two were sub-shedded at Aylesbury, and several were moved away from the London Division in 1956.

Additionally, Southall had 13 of the auto-fitted '54XX' 0-6-0PTs, employed mostly on the Ealing Broadway-West Ruislip 'shuttles' of one or two saloons, while eight of the handy little '14XX' 0-4-2Ts, also auto-fitted, were distributed between Southall, Slough and Reading sheds. They shared duties on the branches with the AEC diesel railcars, but it is worth mentioning that they were similar in size to the little 'Metro' 2-4-0Ts that worked main-line stopping trains prior to the introduction of the '61XXs'!

Various other classes lent a hand, ranging from 'Hall' 4-6-0s on semi-fasts, including those to and from Henley, to the post-war Hawksworth '94XX' 0-6-0PTs, noted on the Henley branch in 1950. In January of that year a '54XX' 0-6-0PT appeared on the Windsor

Western Region: Paddington-Slough (18.5 miles) Weekday down trains			
Year	1948	1966	1994
Traction	Steam	DMUs (first generation)	DMUs ('Network Turbos')
Total (all trains)	53	74	126
No of intermediate stops	10	10	8
Fastest time (mins)	48	45	37
Average speed (mph)	21.8	23.3	28.3
Slowest time (mins)	64	53	41*
Average speed (mph)	17.3	19.8	22.2

* 9 intermediate stops

Mainly confined to the branch lines, the AEC diesel-mechanical railcars played a minor role in the WR London suburban scene. No W21W has ventured on to the Up Relief and is seen passing the goods shed at Southall on 4 April 1959. The vehicle was one of a Swindon-built batch with AEC engines, and the angular style of bodywork applied to those built from 1940 onwards. *F. Hornby*

branch with one auto-trailer, substituting for the usual '61XX' and two coaches.

Personal notes of journeys made in the earlier years mention a 'Hall' leaving platform 2 at Paddington with a 'stopper' to Slough in December 1948, while in March 1949 a '61XX' was found working West Ruislip trains via the Greenford loop. At about the same time pannier tank No 3704 gave a lively performance on a down local – a tribute to the versatility of the small engine, though doubtless hardly popular with the crew! In March 1950 a '54XX' with one auto-trailer was working West Drayton-Uxbridge shuttles, and a year

For a short while after nationalisation a push-pull service operated between Paddington and West Ruislip along the old Birmingham direct line, ceasing with the extension of the Central Line in November 1948. A '54XX' 0-6-0PT of 1931 design propels an auto-saloon through the semi-derelict station at Park Royal, closed since 1937. *Lens of Sutton*

The way it was: purpose-built in the early 1930s for the GWR's London Division suburban services, Collett's '61XX' 2-6-2Ts performed admirably for 30 years on duties such as this, a 'local' seen arriving at Paddington *circa* 1955 with a typical rake of compartment stock. Note the pre-war 'searchlight' signals and the impressive backdrop of Paddington Goods Station. *A. J. Pike*

later a visit was made to Henley-on-Thames behind 0-6-0PT No 5763 with two corridor coaches, the return to Twyford being in the pioneer AEC railcar No W1, built at Southall in 1933.

Another class not generally associated with the London area was the '45XX' small 2-6-2T, but a few of these gravitated to Southall in later years and one of the '55XX' series worked the last train on the Uxbridge (Vine Street) branch in September 1962.

Coaching stock consisted of several groups of non-corridor bogie compartment vehicles, mostly of pre-war build, the oldest of which were the 'Toplight' sets of six 48-foot close-coupled coaches built in 1921 and withdrawn around 1956. Three six-coach articulated sets, also of 48-footers dating from 1925, lasted until 1960. Of the same vintage were rakes of four 57-foot coaches comprising two Brake 3rds and two Composites seating 300 all told, while later sets built in 1931 were made up of flush-sided 60-footers. Further variations were of 1937 design and lasted until 1962, except for some eight-compartment '1sts' that were broken up around 1957; 1st class, incidentally, which had been withdrawn from suburban trains at the outbreak of war, was restored in September 1950, a measure doubtless welcomed by the more affluent commuters.

Post-war vehicles of Hawksworth design included ten-compartment 100-seater 3rds and Brake 3rds, some 100 coaches in all. They were a timely addition to the fleet in view of increasing traffic, though destined for a short life of no more than 11 years. Inevitably a wholesale withdrawal of suburban stock followed dieselisation in 1959-61, including the auto-trailers, among them the batch built as recently as 1951-52. These roomy vehicles attracted some attention in their carmine and cream livery, especially as two were named after birds – 'Thrush' and 'Wren'.

Generally the suburban trains, not infrequently strengthened by a corridor coach, compared favourably for comfort with their contemporaries on some other lines – and indeed, with their diesel successors, in the opinion of many travellers!

The first of the latter into service were Gloucester RCW single cars of the 55000 series (later classified 122), sometimes used with driving trailers, which replaced AEC railcars on the Henley branch in October 1958. They were followed a year later by the 'High Density' sets (Class 117), built by Pressed Steel Co, with two 300 hp Leyland engines giving a maximum speed of 70 mph. The three cars comprised a Driving Motor Brake Second (DMBS), Trailer Composite (TS) and Driving Brake Second (DBS), with doors to each bay and a total seating capacity of 202 2nd and 22 1st Class. The fleet, consisting of 122 vehicles in all, bore the brunt of the London Division suburban duties into the early 1990s, supplemented by the rather more spacious 'Low Density' Metro-Cammell units (Class 101) of identical power and speed capability.

Several variations of driving and trailer cars were produced, forming two-car or three-car sets, capable of working singly or in multiple. A typical three-car formation would seat 158 2nd and 24 1st Class passengers, making them rather more suited to the semi-fast duties, shared with six of the Gloucester RCW 'Cross Country' three-car units, transferred to Reading depot in 1959.

The Pressed Steel single railcars of the 55020 series (Class 121) of 1960 became the logical successors to the auto-trains on the services between Greenford and Ealing Broadway or Paddington as well as on the branches. The DMBSs and the Driving Trailer Seconds (DTS) seat 65 and 91 respectively, and, as their maximum speed of 70 mph matches that of the multiple units, they have also been used in mixed formations with Classes 101 or 117. When first introduced they suffered from braking deficiencies and were temporarily replaced by three-car sets until the problem was solved.

As had happened in steam days, failures resulted in other forms of traction coming to the rescue, as in 1962 when some outer-suburban turns were covered for a week by 'Hymek' diesel-hydraulic locomotives with hauled stock. The final curtain came down on the old order when Southall and Reading closed to steam traction in 1965 and became diesel depots – Reading shed was demolished and replaced by a new building, although the post-

Seen from Paddington's Metropolitan Line platform 15, Class 165/1 'Network Turbo' DMU No 165132 awaits departure on a stopping service to Slough on 15 April 1993. The first appearance of these units on 'Thames Line' duties was precisely one year previously. *F. Hornby*

Hanwell station, comparatively unspoiled and with its 'Great Western' origins still obvious, makes a nice contrast with a brand new Class 166 three-car 'Turbo' DMU on 29 June 1993. The ornamental lamp standards and decorative awnings help to make an attractive picture. *F. Hornby*

war one at Southall survived. In October of that year Southall's allocation consisted of 19 Class 117 units and six Class 121 single cars, with 23 and three respectively at Reading. Four of the Class 117 units were fitted with gangway connections to facilitate ticket issuing and inspection, these being concentrated at Reading. Southall lost its allocation in May 1968, whereafter the whole fleet was based at Reading, joined in October 1982 by new Derby-built experimental three-car diesel-electric unit No 210 001. After extended trials this took over an outer-suburban roster, but the design was not adopted as standard, and No 210 001 was later converted into an electric multiple unit. By March 1986 Reading's allocation totalled 159 vehicles inclusive of 30 Class 117 units, now numbered L400-29.

As further variety, in December 1990 a Class 104 BRCW two-car unit was noted working a special service between Paddington and Hayes & Harlington via the Greenford loop, using the 'rare' curves of both triangle junctions, due to engineering work in the Acton area. It was also reported that an early trip on Sunday mornings from Slough to Paddington was being covered by a London Buses 'midibus', calling at all stations plus Old Oak depot – doubtless for the benefit of staff! By this time the diesel units had been repainted in Network SouthEast livery and sported the 'Thames Line' logo.

It was not until 1992 that the next major change came with the gradual introduction of the Class 165 'Network Turbo' units in April, closely followed by the 165/1 series in two and three-car formations. Two of the latter in multiple unit provide 500 seats in '3+2' layout as compared with 642 seats in ten hauled coaches, and their maximum speed of 90 mph – 20 mph faster than their predecessors – makes them specially welcome in view of the 25 per cent increase in passenger journeys since 1986. Initially they were rostered for the longer runs to Didcot and Oxford, and by 3 January 1992, when the last loco-hauled 'Network Express' left Paddington, there were 25 three-car units available, including some on loan from the Chiltern Line. By the end of the year they were taking over the Reading services from the long-suffering 117s, relegating that class to the branches, but even these last bastions of the 'Heritage' units were under threat when a 'Turbo' took over the Slough-Windsor run at weekends in January 1993. The weekdays 07.32 Henley-Paddington 'Regatta Express' was also entrusted to the newcomers.

In May 1983 the first of the Class 166 variation with 400 hp motors appeared on the scene, and these, with a more roomy '2+2' seating formation and 1st Class accommodation, were allocated to the longer runs, freeing more Class 165s for the stopping services. These commenced operation on the Greenford loop in October 1993, at which time the last preserve of the 117s was on the Marlow branch. With a full complement of 65 'Turbo' units available at Reading depot, 'Driver Only' operating was introduced on 'Thames Line' services in the same month.

In conclusion, we began this survey by commenting on the relatively lowly position held by the Western Region in the 'London commuter league table', but have hopefully charted the steady but impressive transformation that has taken place since 1948. In spite of the loss of the High Wycombe traffic to Marylebone and branch line closures, there are now more trains, well patronised throughout the day, with a fleet of 1990s construction under the control of a thoroughly modernised signalling system. 'Thames Line' is thus well placed to cope with whatever demands the future may hold.

2.
LINES FROM MARYLEBONE

Marylebone-Aylesbury via Amersham
Neasden Junction-Aylesbury via High Wycombe
Wembley Stadium loop

During the early 1990s Marylebone has been tastefully modernised, as befits a station catering for the growing clientele using the new and smartly timed 'Chiltern Line' 'Turbo' trains. Considering that not so long ago it was threatened with closure on more than one occasion, this represents a remarkable turn-round in its fortunes.

When the Great Central (nee Manchester, Sheffield & Lincolnshire) Railway pushed southwards towards the metropolis from Nottingham in 1899 it reached its goal by sharing the existing tracks of the Metropolitan Railway for 42 miles from Quainton Road to Canfield Place, needing only 2 miles of new line for the last lap into its brand new terminus. The fact that the entrepreneurial Sir Edward Watkin was chairman of both companies doubtless greatly facilitated this arrangement, made with the proviso that GCR trains would not call at stations in the 9¼ miles between Harrow and Marylebone, along which stretch two extra tracks were provided for the newcomer.

As the Metropolitan had reached Aylesbury in 1892 and was already offering an adequate service thereto, the prospects for the GCR in building up any worthwhile suburban traffic were clearly limited; indeed, in the earlier years the 13 daily arrivals and departures at Marylebone were all of a 'long-distance' character. But in spite of its fast and comfortable trains between Manchester and London, the competition from three other trunk lines proved too formidable for the newcomer to make a convincing breakthrough and, even many years later, humorists referred to Marylebone station as an 'oasis of peace amidst London's noise and bustle'.

However, in the two decades between the World Wars, the Metropolitan had successfully promoted the advantages of living along its line, under the 'Metroland' banner, which inevitably brought some benefit to the GCR and its LNER successor, as partners on the Aylesbury route. Meanwhile the line through High Wycombe, opened jointly by the GWR and GCR in 1906, had also generated useful traffic. Even in pre-grouping days all 21 of

Seen from the Jubilee Line platform at West Hampstead, a BR train from High Wycombe hurries towards Marylebone on the ex-GCR segregated tracks on 19 July 1986. The down Metropolitan track is between the BR and Jubilee lines, the corresponding up track being out of sight on the far right-hand side. *F. Hornby*

Suburban lines from Marylebone to Aylesbury via Amersham and via High Wycombe and Princes Risborough

Miles	Name	Opened	Closed	Notes
From Marylebone via Amersham				
	Marylebone	3/1899		
9¼	Harrow-on-the-Hill			
13½	Northwood			
17	Rickmansworth			
19¼	Chorley Wood	To GCR traffic		Originally 'Chorley Wood & Chenies'
21½	Chalfont & Latimer	3/1906		
23½	Amersham	(Met & GC		
28¾	Great Missenden	Joint		
33¼	Wendover	Committee)		
35½	Stoke Mandeville			
37¾	Aylesbury			
From Chalfont & Latimer				
3½	Chesham	7/1889		Met Rly
From Marylebone via High Wycombe				
6¼	Wembley Stadium	4/1923	9/1969	Station on loop; last used 8/5/1968
6½	Wembley Stadium	3/1906		'Wembley Hill' to 5/78; 'Wembley Complex' to 5/87
8	Sudbury & Harrow Road	3/1906		
8¾	Sudbury Hill Harrow	3/1906		
9¾	Northolt Park	3/1906		'For Northolt Village' to 6/55
11¼	South Ruislip	1908		
12¼	Ruislip Gardens	1934	7/1958	
13½	West Ruislip	4/1906		Originally 'For Ickenham'
16¼	Denham	4/1906		Originally 'For Harefield'
17	Denham Golf Club Platform	1912		
18¾	Gerrards Cross	4/1906		GW&GC Joint (then GW&LNER Joint)
21½	Seer Green	1915		
23	Beaconsfield	4/1906		Originally 'For Penn'
27¾	High Wycombe	4/1906		Date opened to GC traffic
30	West Wycombe	8/1862	11/1958	
33	Saunderton	8/1862		
36	Princes Risborough	10/1863		
37½	Monks Risborough	11/1929		
39	Little Kimble	6/1872		Originally GWR broad gauge; standard gauge from 10/1868; GW&GC Joint since 1907
42½	South Aylesbury Halt	2/1933	6/1967	
43¼	Aylesbury			

Robinson's handsome 4-6-2Ts were based at Neasden shed for suburban traffic, joined by newly built engines in LNER years so that by nationalisation there were some 30 of the class available. Also, in 1937 the LNER had taken over the responsibility of handling the Metropolitan trains between Rickmansworth and Aylesbury, acquiring most of the motley fleet of steam locomotives from the 'Met' in the process. From the foregoing it can be seen that the suburban services out of Marylebone have always been – both for historical and geographical reasons – very much of an 'outer' nature, Aylesbury being 37¾ miles by one route and 43¼ miles by the other from the London terminus.

During BR years the former GCR line – initially part of the Eastern Region – became something of a political football, passed from one administration to another; the first major upheaval was in July 1949 when Marylebone annexed from Paddington the services to High Wycombe and Princes Risborough via Ruislip.

Then in April 1950 the honours went slightly the other way when Marylebone to Northolt Junction and Neasden to Harrow (exclusive) were transferred to the Western Region, though remaining in the Eastern Region operating area. The London Midland Region gained control eight years later (in February 1958), and in 1963 Marylebone came under LM 'Western Lines' jurisdiction. Meanwhile, as from 11 September 1961 the LMR took over all services north of Amersham from London Transport's Metropolitan line, coincidental with the extension of electrification to that point.

These changes were reflected in the variety of steam motive power employed – fascinating for the enthusiast but surely a headache for the maintenance staff at Neasden shed who, at one time or another, had ER, LMR, WR and BR Standard locomotives under their charge.

In the early 1960s there was a steady and deliberate run-down of the long-distance services culminating in the withdrawal of the few remaining Nottingham semi-fasts on

Although this has the appearance of an outward-bound suburban train, the insignia on the smokebox door of Fairburn Class '4' 2-6-4T No 42256 identifies it as a 'special' heading for the Wembley Stadium loop. It is passing a semaphore-signalled Neasden Junction on 2 May 1959 – Cup Final day! *B. W. Brooksbank*

5 September 1966, after which the line beyond Aylesbury was closed to passenger traffic. The Marylebone to Aylesbury direct route was thus left with only the 'outer-suburbans', dieselised since 1961, so that the situation was thus exactly the opposite of that in the early GCR years. Nevertheless uncertainty persisted, with proposals in 1969 to divert trains on the High Wycombe line back to Paddington, leaving Baker Street to deal with all Aylesbury traffic, while the Neasden to Northolt Junction link would close. Reprieve came after due consideration in 1972, on the grounds of hardship to passengers using the four threatened stations, plus the expenditure that would be incurred, but by 1984 Marylebone was once again under sentence of closure. This time it was the extra revenue generated by the introduction of Travel Cards that saved the day, and the closure notice was eventually withdrawn in April 1986.

Next came regional boundary changes from 11 October 1987, whereby Marylebone-Aynho Junction via High Wycombe, Neasden Junction-Claydon Junction via Aylesbury, and Greenford-Northolt Junction were transferred from the London Midland to the Western Region. By this time 'Network SouthEast' had been launched, and plans were laid for the replacement of the ageing fleet of diesel units and for improvements to Marylebone station. While work on tracks and signalling was in progress trains were indeed diverted into Paddington in fulfilment of the 1969 proposals, but only on Sundays and only temporarily!

Routes and infrastructure

See the map on page 10-11.

Historically the services out of Marylebone make use of stations of Metropolitan and Great Western Railway origin on the Aylesbury direct route and the line via High Wycombe respectively, with only the four stations between the Neasden and Northolt Junctions, plus the terminus itself, built exclusively for GCR purposes.

Hidden behind the imposing frontage of a hotel building – latterly headquarters of the British Railways Board – Marylebone station is of modest proportions and its four platform faces are adequate, even today with more trains in and out than ever before. It has recently been extensively modernised, and a booking office on the concourse – perhaps more convenient but less imposing than the original – doubles for BR and for London Underground's Bakerloo Line below.

A new 60-lever mechanical signal box came into use in 1967 controlling the station, the approaches and access to the diesel depot. Colour-light signalling was installed in September/October 1990 and stabling sidings for the 'Turbo' trains were provided on the west side, at which time the diesel depot closed.

Half a mile or so out of the station the lines plunge into a series of shallow tunnels beneath St John's Wood and Lord's cricket ground (fulfilling a solemn pledge that the coming of the railway would not desecrate the sacred pitch!) before climbing up alongside the Metropolitan and Jubilee lines near Finchley Road. The 'Chiltern Line' tracks remain independent out to Harrow-on-the-Hill, beyond which the double track to Rickmansworth was shared by BR and Metropolitan trains until quadrupling took place between 1959 and 1962. Thereafter one pair has been allotted to BR and to Metropolitan fast trains, leaving the other tracks free for Metropolitan stopping services. Passing Neasden the site of the former steam shed (closed in 1966) can be seen on the down side, closely followed by the divergence of the link line to Northolt Junction.

Harrow-on-the-Hill, 9¼ miles from Marylebone, is the first stop for 'Chiltern Line' trains. The station was reconstructed in stages by London Transport between 1938 and 1948 and has six platform faces, providing interchange with the Metropolitan Line. A busy bus station in the yard makes it an admirable centre for rail and road public transport.

Onwards from Harrow the fast lines bypass the next four stations out to Moor Park, noted for its golf courses. Beyond here the four tracks merge into two between the South and North Junctions for the Metropolitan branch to Watford.

Rebuilding at Aylesbury is well advanced on 30 May 1991 as a Class 115 DMU awaits departure time alongside the new signal box. The unit, in NSE livery, bears the name *Aylesbury College, Silver Jubilee 1987* on the leading power car. *F. Hornby*

When the Neasden-Northolt Junction line was opened the stations were quite lavish, in expectation of building development at a later date. Although now surrounded by housing they have been drastically 'rationalised' – as evidenced by this view of the rebuilt Sudbury & Harrow Road on 18 January 1994, the new island platform occupying the site of the former through roads. The 'Turbo' unit on a service from High Wycombe has not deigned to stop! *F. Hornby*

Then comes Rickmansworth, currently the second stopping place out of Marylebone, at the foot of a 7-mile climb through Chalfont & Latimer to Amersham. Chalfont is the junction for a 4-mile Metropolitan single-track branch to Chesham, on which, prior to electrification in August 1960, shuttle services were worked by a BR steam locomotive with Metropolitan stock. Amersham, a town of 17,000 inhabitants, became the outer terminus for Metropolitan services in September 1960. From here there are only three stations in the remaining rather thinly populated 14 miles to Aylesbury. From a summit between Great Missenden and Wendover it is downhill at 1 in 117 over the final 7 miles.

Aylesbury, the county town of Buckinghamshire, has grown considerably in post-war years and now has 50,000 inhabitants. The station has been modernised without seriously interfering with its traditional architecture, and a new depot has been built nearby where the 'Turbo' diesel units are maintained. There is, however, no trace of the small two-road steam shed that once occupied a site alongside the station on the down side.

Until recent years much of the direct route to Aylesbury was still mechanically signalled, save that a new box controlling colour-lights came into use at Amersham in 1960. The semaphores have now made way for three-aspect colour-lights, and a power box has been commissioned on the platform at the London end of Aylesbury station. The maximum line speed has been upgraded to 75 mph, to the benefit of the 'Turbo' units.

To consider the other route to Aylesbury, via High Wycombe, we must retrace our steps to

Neasden, where it branches off the direct route to link, 6½ miles further on, with the ex-GWR line from Paddington by a flying junction at Northolt. There are four stations between the two junctions, only two of which – Wembley Stadium and Northolt Park – are now served outside peak hours. This stretch is not unlike its near neighbour, the WR Greenford loop, in its urban surroundings, though the stations as built were – unnecessarily as it turned out – far more lavish and have been much simplified in recent years.

At least passing notice should also be taken of the Wembley Stadium loop, which, although concerned only with special events, made heavy demands on suburban stock and motive power on those occasions. The loop, about a mile in length, diverged at Neasden North Junction from the Northolt Junction line, which it rejoined, facing Neasden, some 600 yards further on. The special trains, running at intervals of only a few minutes when required, traversed it in a clockwise direction, calling at the single-platform Stadium station before doubling back to Marylebone. It had opened in April 1923 in time for the first FA Cup Final, and closed in September 1969.

From Northolt Junction through High Wycombe to Princes Risborough we are on the erstwhile GWR&GCR Joint line of 1906, which received due notice in the previous chapter by virtue of the fact that for a short while after nationalisation it was served by stopping trains from Paddington as well as from Marylebone. Though undulating, the line is easily graded with a summit near Beaconsfield, and some of the long-distance expresses from Marylebone took this route,

After a major football match this platform at Wembley Stadium would have been thronged with jubilant (or disappointed) crowds awaiting transport back to Marylebone. No doubt due to the increasing popularity of road transport, the station and loop closed in September 1969. *Lens of Sutton*

West Ruislip station on the one-time GW&GCR Joint line still displays a strong GWR influence, on the up platform at least. This view towards High Wycombe shows the modern overbridge linking the 'Chiltern Line' station with the Central Line terminus on the left-hand side. *F. Hornby*

which had the advantage of avoiding possible delays from Metropolitan trains.

Most off-peak trains make eight stops in the 28 miles to and from High Wycombe, about half as many as in a comparable distance from Liverpool Street or Victoria, emphasising the contrast in the catchment areas served. South and West Ruislip became interchange stations when the Central Line extension was completed in November 1948. Beyond Ruislip the line crosses the River Colne, then reaches Beaconsfield, with 13,000 inhabitants, and High Wycombe itself, a sprawling conurbation of 70,000 souls, both places contributing their valuable quotas of daily commuters.

The station layout at High Wycombe was duly 'rationalised' during May 1990, when the centre roads were removed and replacement of the many GWR-type semaphore signals began. The up and down platforms here are staggered, with a terminal bay at the London end of the down platform, long enough for a pair of two-car diesel units.

All told, inclusive of station refurbishments between West Ruislip and High Wycombe and the removal of mechanical signal boxes, some £70 million has been expended on a thorough-going modernisation programme.

From High Wycombe there are now only four stations in the remaining 15½ miles to Aylesbury, two others – West Wycombe and South Aylesbury Halt – having been closed in 1958 and 1967 respectively. There is a rising gradient from High Wycombe to Saunderton, then a fairly steep fall, on average at 1 in 100. For some 3 miles beyond Saunderton the up and down lines diverge, the latter being the 1862 original while the up line was laid in the early 1900s. They come together again at Princes Risborough, the second of the stations still open.

Princes Risborough was in its heyday the junction for a branch to Watlington and for a secondary line to Oxford via Thame, which lost their passenger services in 1961 and 1963 respectively. The mechanical signalling equipment here, rendered redundant by the installation of MAS (multiple-aspect signalling) has been acquired by a local preservation association.

The main line onwards to Banbury and Birmingham is of course still open and used by the hourly service to and from Marylebone, but we turn due north along the remaining sparsely populated 7 miles to Aylesbury. This is single track across mainly flat country and of Great Western origin, albeit originally opened in 1863 by the independent Wycombe Railway. There is a descent at 1 in 50 beyond Little Kimble, the second of the two stations, and the direct route via Amersham is joined close to Aylesbury station.

Services

For some years following nationalisation in 1948, so long as steam traction prevailed there was no great change in the services on the Aylesbury direct line, either in speed or frequency. As an example of the prevailing standards, the 1953 timetable showed only 11 weekday stopping trains each way, taking from 88 to 101 minutes for the 37¾ miles with from eight to ten stops en route. Other than a solitary through train from Chesham for the early risers, the first arrival at Marylebone was at 08.51 from Aylesbury, closely followed by a faster train taking only 80 minutes with two fewer stops. However, travellers from the county town in those days also had the benefit of five fast trains originating from Woodford or points further north, with an average journey time of 1 hour.

The Saturday frequency was similar, but with adjustments, mainly in the down direction, to allow for the half-day, while on Sundays there were just two stopping and two fast trains. On this route, of course, the Metropolitan also provided a frequent service to and from Baker Street and the City.

The line via High Wycombe fared rather better, thanks to the transfer of most services from Paddington to Marylebone in 1949. In the up direction off-peak trains, inclusive of five through from Princes Risborough, left High Wycombe at 10 minutes past each hour, all stations to West Ruislip then non-stop into Marylebone. Stopping trains from West Ruislip followed 10 minutes later, taking 35 minutes for the 13½ miles, but these were severely

Class 'A5' 4-6-2T No 69805, a Gorton product of 1911, eases into Marylebone on 10 October 1953 with a stopping train from Aylesbury comprised of Gresley stock. Although transferred away from Neasden shortly afterwards, No 69805 remained in service until September 1959. *F. Hornby*

curtailed from January 1951, with some trains from High Wycombe making extra stops in partial compensation. Despite the growth of housing along this section over the years, it undoubtedly suffers from the close proximity of stations on the Piccadilly Line.

In the 1953 timetable, inclusive of two trains through from Aylesbury and nine from Princes Risborough, there were 31 weekday up trains all told from High Wycombe, ranging from 53 minutes with six stops to 68 minutes with 12 stops, for the 27¾ miles. The Sunday service consisted of 17 trains, of which six were through from Princes Risborough and one from Brackley.

Five years later, the pattern in the 1958/59 Winter timetable was substantially unchanged on both lines, but dieselisation was looming on the horizon, a trial run having been made by a two-car unit between Marylebone and Beaconsfield as far back as April 1954. The phasing out of steam traction began on 23 January 1961, a process completed for stopping trains on both routes by June of the following year. During the interim stages the new four-car

diesel mechanical sets ran to steam-train timings, but with the completion of track quadrupling between Harrow and Watford South Junction, improvements were possible. Hitherto a few BR trains had called at stations between Harrow-on-the Hill and Rickmansworth, but this was no longer possible as only Moor Park had extra platforms on the new fast lines, for the benefit of Metropolitan trains only.

From 18 June 1961, therefore, all BR services were non-stop over this section, with hourly off-peak trains on weekdays and Saturdays to and from Aylesbury making seven stops with a 59-minute schedule. Frequency was stepped up to quarter-hourly during peak times, the total number of trains being double that of steam days, while the running time was reduced, on average, by half an hour. On Sundays there were still only two through trains in each direction, but others shuttled between Aylesbury and Amersham, connecting there with the Metropolitan services.

Initially on the High Wycombe line the diesel units showed less superiority over their steam

The cars on the left may give some clue as to the period of this photograph, as does the blue-grey livery, but the Derby-built Class 115 DMU could have been seen here at Marylebone at any time during three decades. The date is actually 30 March 1984, and the absence of passengers confirms, as does the distant clock, that this is an 'off-peak' scene. *F. Hornby*

predecessors, due to the numerous service slacks, so the average schedule of 53 minutes between High Wycombe and Marylebone was only marginally better than the fastest trains in 1953. Nevertheless the hourly interval service with extras at business times, plus the restoration of hourly stopping trains to and from West Ruislip, represented an overall improvement. Beyond High Wycombe some additional services were extended through to and from Aylesbury in 1962.

In the introductory diesel year of 1961 just 49 trains left Marylebone on weekdays, carrying some 6,000 passengers. By 1968 the total number of arrivals and departures had risen to 126, all now operating within the confines of the two routes to Aylesbury, as long-distance services had ceased two years previously.

During the remaining years in which the Derby four-car sets kept their monopoly the level of services remained fairly constant. Taking 1966 as an example, there were 26 down trains to Aylesbury on weekdays and Saturdays, calling at Harrow and all stations to Rickmansworth, while on Sundays 16 trains each way between Amersham and Aylesbury ran in connection with Metropolitan services. On the High Wycombe line there were 35 weekday down trains, ten of which went on to Princes Risborough and six more to Aylesbury. The Saturday and Sunday timetables showed 24 and 17 departures respectively, the journey time to High Wycombe being little changed at

50 minutes. Ten years later, as part of a London Midland Region economy drive, some service cuts were made as from 5 January 1976.

Moving on to the present day, following the introduction of the 'Network Turbo' diesel units, we find that Marylebone has regained something of its main-line status by virtue of the fact that in 1993 there are seven trains through to Birmingham (Snow Hill), all but one of which make three stops before High Wycombe. The off-peak pattern is for a stopping train to High Wycombe at 10 minutes past each hour and a fast train at 40 minutes past, continuing alternately to Banbury and Birmingham. There are trains to and from Aylesbury on this route at peak times only, with off-peak shuttles between Aylesbury and Princes Risborough and – as a reminder of bygone days – a morning train through from Paddington! All told, on weekdays High Wycombe sees 48 arrivals from Marylebone, while another seven provide a morning and evening service as far as Gerrards Cross only. The 'Turbo' trains have reduced the journey time to High Wycombe to 44 minutes with eight stops.

On the Aylesbury direct route, in addition to two early morning workings between Amersham and Aylesbury, there are 34 through trains on weekdays taking 55-56 minutes, eight more than in the 1960s with a slight reduction in journey times. The Sunday service is similarly improved, with 25 trains plying between Amersham and Aylesbury.

Traction and trains

The first suburban services out of Marylebone in 1906 were worked by the then new GCR 4-4-2Ts, a few of which survived at Neasden well into the 1950s, mainly for the Chesham branch, but they were displaced from main-line duties by the imposing 'A5' 4-6-2Ts from 1911 onwards. In 1948 these locomotives were still the mainstay on both routes, but their decline was rapid after the appearance of Thompson's 'L1' 2-6-4Ts in that year, and the last two 'A5s' were transferred away from Neasden in mid-1954.

The GCR had provided four-coach bogie sets for the London area suburban trains, superior to most of their contemporaries, but in LNER days Gresley compartment stock gradually appeared on the scene. The normal loads consisted of five or six non-corridor bogies, well within the capabilities of the powerful six-coupled locomotives. Later, some 1940-built twin-articulated sets were also in use.

The effects of nationalisation were soon felt and in May 1949 a Fairburn 2-6-4T of LMS design appeared on High Wycombe duties. In July of that year a shortage of 'A5s' and 'L1s' due to maintenance arrears led to such varied types being pressed into service as 'J11' 0-6-0s, 'N2' and 'N7' 0-6-2Ts, Fowler and Stanier 2-6-4Ts (on loan from the LM Region), 'B1' 4-6-0s, and even a 'V2' 2-6-2. Also noted at this time were a pair of WR '61XX' 2-6-2Ts, sub-shedded at Aylesbury and frequently working through to Marylebone. By 1950 Neasden's allocation of 'L1s' was no fewer than 37, with the 'A5s' correspondingly reduced to five.

The stopping trains between Marylebone and West Ruislip were worked by 'N5' 0-6-2Ts of GCR origin and – after 1949 – by five 'N7' 0-6-2Ts fitted with vacuum-controlled push-pull gear. These engines also saw service on the Chesham branch, but were transferred away to King's Cross shed after the curtailment of the West Ruislip trains in January 1951.

Gresley's 'Quad-art' (four-coach articulated sets) also saw some use on this service from 1949, and were also noted, hauled by 'A5s' and 'L1s', on specials to Wembley Stadium for the 1950 Amateur Cup Final.

On a journey made to West Ruislip on 16 September 1950 a down semi-fast consisted of six coaches hauled by 'L1' No 67782, and the return on a stopping train had 'N5' No 9302 as motive power. This particular engine, still with its LNER number, was not auto-fitted, so a smart 'run round' had to be made at West Ruislip. An 'A5' 4-6-2T was noted similarly employed, but there was no sign of the 'N7s' on this occasion. As late as 1955 the ageing 'N5s' were still hard at work on the remaining West Ruislip turns.

In 1951 the ACV diesel set of three four-wheelers appeared at Marylebone and some trial runs were made on the Chesham branch before they were moved elsewhere – no doubt to the great relief of the patrons!

Although nominally powerful engines, the

Typical of the run-down state of many locomotives in steam's last years, a filthy BR Class '4' 2-6-0 rests at the buffers at Marylebone on 1 July 1961. The six coaches of compartment stock are representative of former GCR line stopping trains over many years. *B. W. Brooksbank*

Above The six-road diesel servicing depot at Marylebone on 16 May 1978, during the 'Rail Blue' livery era. Two of the 30 Class 115 DMUs allocated here await their next assignments. *F. Hornby*

Right On 22 April 1992 brand new Class 165 two-car 'Turbo' unit No '65019' hurries through Moor Park en route from Aylesbury to Marylebone. After 30 years of 'High Density' Class 115s, the newcomers, with their 'next station' display screens and superior seating, represent a decided improvement. *F. Hornby*

'L1s' were prone to failures, frequently due to hot axle-boxes, and in 1954 a critical situation was resolved by the transfer from the Tilbury section of Fairburn 2-6-4Ts, which remained on the strength until dieselisation. By 1957 Neasden's 'L1' allocation had dwindled to 17, and to a mere two within another year. In mid-1956 a batch of new BR Standard 2-6-4Ts (Nos 80137-44) also arrived, and a visit to Neasden shed in March 1957 produced 12 'L1s', nine Fairburns and five BR Standard 2-6-4Ts, with two 'C14' 4-4-2Ts keeping up the old GCR tradition. Also present were three BR Class '4' 2-6-0s, which were not infrequently used on semi-fast passenger turns.

All this changed dramatically from 1961 onwards with the introduction of the Derby-built four-car diesel mechanical units of 1960 construction – later classified 115. With two 460 hp BUT engines per unit and a maximum speed of 70 mph, they were of 'High Density' design, similar to the contemporary Western Region Class '117s', seating 302 2nd and 30 1st Class passengers per unit. In 1962 a six-road maintenance depot was constructed for them just outside Marylebone station on the up side, and this remained in use for 30 years until the coming of the 'Turbos'. At the other end of the line, units are also stabled in the purpose-built depot at Aylesbury.

The Marylebone depot allocation in 1965 consisted of 30 Class 115 four-car units. A 1968 survey revealed that there were variations within that class, most certainly as regards livery, which, basically at that time, was 'Rail Blue'. Some had yellow panels and others full yellow ends, with the emblems on cab doors or body sides and with two different sizes of numerals!

During the 1970s and 1980s the allocation remained more or less constant, but from May 1986 the fleet was repainted in 'Network SouthEast' livery, and in June 1987 one of the driving vehicles received the name *Aylesbury College, Silver Jubilee 1987* – a first for a DMU.

In December 1989 orders were placed with BREL for the 'Network Turbo' units, and the first of Class 165 was due into service in February 1991, with a complete complement of 89 vehicles scheduled by September; however, it was not until 4 May that No 165001 made a brief appearance at Marylebone. These two- and three-car units are powered by two Perkins 350 bhp engines, giving a maximum speed of 90 mph, and are the first to be fitted with 'SELCAB' Automatic Train Protection. On 'Chiltern Line' services they display two-character headcodes between 01 and 19.

Meantime, doubtless with the 115s becoming progressively run down, Class 47 locomotives with five Mk I coaches were drafted into service on the Aylesbury direct route during November 1990. There were in fact still a few turns on this line covered by 115s at the end of 1991 due to the new units having clearance problems at Rickmansworth, but this was resolved by 20 January 1992. Some Class 165s were based at Old Oak for a time, pending full use of the new Aylesbury depot, and a 'last run' was made by a Class 115 on the 20.45 service from Aylesbury on 29 July 1992, so bringing to an end an era lasting 31 years.

3.
METROPOLITAN RAILWAY

Aldgate and Baker Street to Amersham, Watford, Chesham, Uxbridge and Aylesbury

The Metropolitan Railway had its origins in a 3¾-mile line between Farringdon Street in the City and Bishops Road, Paddington, opened in January 1863. Years later, with aspirations to become a 'main-line' company, it reached out into Buckinghamshire, to Chesham in 1889 and Aylesbury in 1892. Its outer limit was Verney Junction on the Bletchley-Oxford line, but passenger services to this outpost ceased in 1936.

It was over Metropolitan metals, southwards from Quainton Road, that the Great Central Railway came to town in 1899, sharing the

See the map on page 10-11.

double track for 42 miles until quadrupling took place out to Harrow-on-the-Hill, and eventually to Watford South Junction in 1959-62. The Baker Street-Harrow section was electrified in 1905 and extended in stages to Rickmansworth, together with a new branch to Watford in 1925. Traffic into 'Metroland' grew, and there was even a daily Pullman service until the outbreak of war in September 1939. Steam traction was employed north of Rickmansworth; the 'Met' steam locomotives were taken over by the LNER in 1937, but were displaced from passenger duties during the war. After nationalisation BR steam locomotives were employed until the third and fourth rails

Were it not for the London Transport 'bullseye' on the left, this scene at Chesham could be mistaken for a country branch line far from the capital. Ex-GCR Class 'C14' 4-4-2T No 67418 is in charge of the Chesham-Chalfont shuttle on 29 September 1956. *F. Hornby*

Metropolitan Railway

Miles	Name	Opened	Closed	Notes
Miles from Aldgate				
	Aldgate	11/1876		
½	Liverpool Street*	7/1875		
¾	Moorgate*	12/1865		'Moorgate Street' to 10/1924
3	King's Cross/St Pancras*	1/1863		
4½	Baker Street**	4/1863		
6½	Finchley Road**	1879		
11	Wembley Park	1894		
12	Preston Road	1908		
13	Northwick Park	1923		Originally '& Kenton'
14	Harrow-on-the-Hill*	8/1880		
15	North Harrow	3/1915		
16	Pinner	5/1885		
17¼	Northwood Hills	11/1933		
18¼	Northwood	9/1887		
19½	Moor Park	5/1910	Met & GC Joint from 1906	Originally 'Sandy Lodge', then 'Moor Park & Sandy Lodge'
21½	Rickmansworth*	9/1887		
24	Chorley Wood*	1889		
26¼	Chalfont & Latimer*	1889		'Chalfont Road' to 11/1915
28¼	Amersham	9/1892		
42½	Aylesbury	9/1892		
From Moor Park/Rickmansworth				
1½	Croxley	1/1925		
2¼	Watford	1/1925		
From Chalfont & Latimer				
3½	Chesham	7/1889		Met & GC Joinnt from 1906
From Harrow-on-the-Hill				
½	West Harrow	1913		
1½	Rayners Lane	1906		Station rebuilt 1937
2½	Eastcote	1906		
3¼	Ruislip Manor	1912		Station rebuilt 1938
3¾	Ruislip	7/1904		
5	Ickenham	1905		
5½	Hillingdon	1923		
7	Uxbridge	7/1904		

* Interchange with BR station
** Metropolitan stations between Baker Street and Finchley Road closed 1939/40

were extended to Amersham and Chesham in September 1961. Thereafter the stations beyond Amersham have been served exclusively by BR trains in and out of Marylebone.

A visit to Chesham in December 1950 produced an ex-GCR 'N5' 0-6-2T, which gave a lively run on the branch, with 'L1' 2-6-4Ts working between Aylesbury and Rickmans-

A southbound Metropolitan train formed of two 'A60' units hurries through Neasden on 26 January 1985. The Jubilee Line tracks are in the foreground, and just north of the station are the extensive car sheds and sidings where much of the 'Met' fleet is stabled and serviced. *F. Hornby*

Croxley is the only intermediate station on the Metropolitan line's Watford branch, with a stylish brick building on the overbridge dating from 1925. A down train of 'A60' stock is seen there on 1 July 1989, on which day the branch was also host to a WR 0-6-0PT and 'Met' electric loco *Sarah Siddons* on specials. *F. Hornby*

worth, where they handed over to Metropolitan electric locomotives. On another visit in 1956 a 'C14' 4-4-2T worked the branch train, which still consisted of three Metropolitan ex-electric coaches; Fairburn 2-6-4Ts were responsible for the main-line trains north of Rickmansworth. By then the electric locomotives sported their original names and crimson liveries. By the late 1950s Ivatt Class '2' 2-6-2Ts had taken over on the Chesham branch and one of these, No 41284, was in charge of the last steam train on 11 September 1960.

Baker Street Metropolitan station, over-shadowed by the impressive bulk of Chiltern Court, took its present form in 1912, with the four-track through station just below the surface and the platforms for Hammersmith & City and Circle Line trains at a slightly lower level. Beneath these are the Bakerloo and Jubilee Line 'tubes'.

The Metropolitan and Jubilee Lines emerge into the open at Finchley Road where there is cross-platform interchange, and the two keep company to Wembley Park, where the Jubilee diverges to Stanmore. Since the quadrupling, interchange between Metropolitan and BR services has been restricted to Harrow-on-the-Hill, Rickmansworth and the stations thence to Amersham.

One can only presume that there are fewer vandals to the square mile in 'Metroland' than in many other areas, as the stations (if not the trains) are graffiti-free and well maintained – many even with accessible toilets! Watford and Croxley, dating from 1925, are excellent examples of the architecture of that period.

Twenty 1,200 hp Bo-Bo electric locomotives were built in 1904/06 and extensively rebuilt in 1922/23 by Metropolitan-Vickers. From 1925 they spent most of their working lives on

Above Metropolitan Bo-Bo electric locomotive No 3 *Sir Ralph Verney* is seen at Baker Street on 4 June 1961 ready to take an Aylesbury train as far as Rickmansworth. There were 20 of these fine machines, rebuilt into the form as shown in 1922/23 and restored to their pre-war maroon livery during the 1950s. *F. Hornby*

Left Before the 1959-61 widening Moor Park station boasted two platforms with rather primitive shelters. On 27 October 1956 a train of 1927-built 'T' stock calls there en route from Watford to Aldgate. These rather elegant teak-coloured units were retired from service in October 1962. *F. Hornby*

Left Wembley Park is one of those latter-day London Transport stations apparently designed solely with a T-square! On 13 December 1987 the footbridge frames a train of Metropolitan 'A60' stock en route from Watford to Baker Street. *F. Hornby*

LONDON COMMUTER LINES

passenger trains between Baker Street or the City and Rickmansworth, with one daily through working each way on the Watford branch. For a brief period around 1960 they also worked through trains to and from Chesham, but the majority were withdrawn in 1962. One survivor, No 12 *Sarah Siddons*, makes frequent appearances on special trains and has been seen as far afield as the South Coast!

In 1948 the off-peak service between Baker Street and Aylesbury consisted of two trains hourly at irregular intervals, the standard journey time for the 38 miles being 87 minutes with nine stops; 4 minutes were allowed for the changeover between electric and steam traction at Rickmansworth. At peak times the trains ran through to and from Liverpool Street, adding about 13 minutes to the end-to-end time.

The Watford services were operated by 'T' stock multiple units introduced in 1927, in six-coach formations enhanced to eight coaches at busy times. The motor-coaches were powered by four 275 hp motors producing a maximum speed of 60 mph (5 mph less than the locomotives). The off-peak service consisted of four trains per hour between Watford and Baker Street, allowed 41 minutes with 11 stops. At peak times they ran through to and from Aldgate.

The major works of 1959-61, extending electrification to Amersham and Chesham, heralded the withdrawal of the 'T' stock and the appearance of 62 new four-car units of 'A60' stock in silver-grey livery. Since 1981 all trains save for the Chesham shuttle service have consisted of two such units.

From the introduction of a completely new timetable on 18 June 1962 the off-peak service has consisted of half-hourly trains between Aldgate and Amersham, and quarter-hourly between Baker Street and Watford – extended to Aldgate, as before, at peak times. The Amersham trains are allowed 43 minutes beyond Baker Street with six stops – 13 minutes less than in 1948 – but the Watford service is only marginally faster.

Additionally to these routes, the Harrow-Uxbridge branch, electrified in 1905, had trains every 15 minutes off-peak in 1948 with a 40-minute schedule (reduced by 2 minutes in the 1990s). Between Ruislip and Ickenham on this branch, a spur gives access to the Central Line depot at West Ruislip, alongside the BR High Wycombe line. The final section from Rayners Lane to Uxbridge is shared with Piccadilly Line trains at peak hours.

The track widening northwards from Harrow-on-the-Hill involved considerable infrastructure changes, with platforms lengthened at several stations and extensive rebuilding at Northwood, Moor Park and Amersham. Many bridges were reconstructed and the signalling system was improved, including provision of a new box at Amersham. The local lines are controlled by two-aspect colour-light signals and the fast lines by three-aspects, as is also the double track section beyond Rickmansworth.

In conclusion it is of interest to note that the Metropolitan Line beyond Northwood was subject to a swingeing fare increase of 40 per cent in July 1977 when local County Council grants were not forthcoming. As examples of the effects of inflation at that period, this was followed, throughout the LT system, by rises of 10 per cent in June 1978, 8 per cent in June 1979, 12-13 per cent in September and another 19 per cent in March 1980!

4.
LINES FROM EUSTON

In two of the previous chapters we have been concerned with steam-hauled suburban services that were dieselised during BR years, but in turning to the lines out of Euston we encounter a fascinating combination of steam, diesel, DC and AC electric traction.

Like the Great Western, the London & North Western Railway, as successor to the London & Birmingham, was essentially a 'main-line' company in its early years, with little expectation of worthwhile revenue from the few stations serving small communities south of Watford. Indeed, in 1841 all but two of the 13 daily departures from Euston were for Rugby and beyond, but some modest development took place along the line in the 1860s as far out as Harrow. Later, with four tracks available since 1875, some kind of local service was deemed necessary and, from June 1879, hourly trains were provided between Euston and Watford. A census in 1903 showed 36 daily suburban arrivals at Euston and, during the Edwardian decade, Webb's 2-4-2Ts and 0-6-2Ts were replaced by Whales's 4-4-2 'Precursor tanks' with neat rakes of bogie stock – evidence of the increasing importance of this traffic.

Willesden Junction was rebuilt in 1894 and two additional tracks – the 'New Lines' – were completed through it from Kensal Green to Watford in February 1913, along which new stations were opened, with additional platforms at the existing ones. The planned electric services from Euston could not commence until two new single-line tunnels were completed at Primrose Hill and, with the intervention of the First World War, this was delayed until July 1922. In the meantime it fell to the Bakerloo line to operate the first electric trains along the New Lines, from Queens Park to Willesden Junction on 10 May 1915, and on to Watford Junction on weekdays in April 1917, joined in the peak hours by a few LNWR trains from Broad Street.

Within months of the start of the Euston-Watford electric service the LNWR became the largest constituent of the newly formed LMS, but the three-car multiple units, designed originally for the 1914 Willesden-Earls Court service, were still at work 25 years later when the LMS was in turn absorbed by British Railways. During those years electrification had stimulated housing developments along the line, with the fortunate residents enjoying a frequent service not only to Euston but also to Broad Street, and by Bakerloo tube via the West End to the Elephant & Castle.

On the parallel main line the outer limit for residential services had moved steadily further from London, out to Tring and Bletchley, and from 1928 onwards the new Fowler 2-6-4Ts were able to show their paces on the smartly timed semi-fasts. By 1948 the standard of service was not far short of that on offer prior to the outbreak of war in September 1939.

DC LINES
Euston-Watford, Croxley Green & Rickmansworth, including Bakerloo Line from Queens Park

Routes and infrastructure

Until the comprehensive reconstruction of 1963-68, Euston could almost rival the old Waterloo of LSWR days in being a haphazard collection of train sheds, resulting from piecemeal additions over the years. Prior to rebuilding, the tracks at platforms 4, 5 and 7 were electrified for the DC trains, but in the modernised station two platforms, Nos 9 and 10, are deemed adequate, the three-car units appearing rather insignificant under the vast expanse of roof.

Once clear of the platforms the up and down slow lines are shared by AC and DC trains for a mile or so until the latter diverge on to their own tracks at Chalk Farm. Here they descend by a burrowing junction graded at 1 in 37 to re-emerge on the up (north) side of the main lines, where they are joined by a spur from the North London line, now 'freight only' but formerly used by the electric trains between Broad Street and Watford. They then pass through the twin-bore 1,220-yard Primrose Hill Tunnel and the stations at South Hampstead and Kilburn High Road, both with booking offices on overbridges at the western ends. Next is Queens Park, where the Bakerloo line surfaces between the up and down DC tracks at the London end of the station, which consists of two island platforms spanned by a wide glass canopy.

After threading the twin-bore Kensal Rise Tunnel the DC and main lines part company, with Willesden Traction & Maintenance Depot for electric and diesel locomotives between the two on a site formerly occupied by carriage sheds. The 'New Lines' Willesden New station consists of a wide island platform with two bays inset, which, in the early days were for the benefit of trains terminating there, but one track has been removed and the other sees little use. There are footbridges at both ends of the

---

Suburban lines from Euston:
DC lines from Euston to Watford Junction and branches

Miles	Name	Opened (New Lines)	Closed	Notes
From Euston				
0	Euston			
2½	South Hampstead	7/1922		Original main line station 1879
3¼	Kilburn High Road	7/1922		Original main line station 1851
3¾	Queens Park	2/1915		'Queens Park (West Kilburn)' to 12/1954
4½	Kensal Green	10/1916		
5½	Willesden Junction (New)	6/1912		
5⅞	Harlesden	6/1912		
7½	Stonebridge Park	6/1912		
8¼	Wembley Central	6/1912		'For Sudbury'
8¾	North Wembley	6/1912		
9½	South Kenton	7/1933		
10¼	Kenton	6/1912		
11½	Harrow & Wealdstone	6/1912		
12¾	Headstone Lane	2/1913		
13½	Hatch End	6/1912		'For Pinner' to 6/1956
14¾	Carpenders Park	1914		New station opened 1953
16	Bushey	2/1913		'Bushey & Oxhey'
16¾	Watford High Street	2/1913		
17¾	Watford Junction	2/1913		
Croxley Green and Rickmansworth branches				
	Watford Junction			
1½	Watford (FC station)	12/1982		⎫
2	Watford West	6/1912		⎬ Electrified from 10/1922
2¼	Croxley Green	6/1912		⎭
3½	Rickmansworth Church Street	10/1862	3/1952	Electrified from 9/1927

LONDON COMMUTER LINES

LINES FROM EUSTON

Main line
DC lines

Watford west
Croxley Green
To Aylesbury
Rickmansworth

Met&GCR

To Harrow

Bushey

Watford Junction

Carpenders Park

Hatch End

Headstone Lane

Harrow & Wealstone

Kenton

South Kenton

North Wembley

To Neasden

Met&GCR

Belmont

Stanmore Village

To Harrow

To Northolt Junction

GCR

Wembley Central

Stonebridge Park

Harlesden

To Neasden

See enlargement above

EUSTON

Queens Park station on 14 August 1985 with a Watford-bound Class 501 three-car EMU in blue-grey livery. The 501s were Eastleigh-built in 1957-8 in line with contemporary Southern Region designs, save that screw couplings were fitted in place of buckeyes. The Bakerloo Line platforms are just visible on the left, with the main lines on the right. *F. Hornby*

Above Kensal Green is typical of most of the DC line stations between Euston and Willesden Junction, with the booking office spanning the tracks. In this view on 23 August 1992 a southbound Bakerloo Line train of 1972 Mk II stock is emerging from the short twin-bore tunnel. *F. Hornby*

Left Willesden New Station on 17 August 1988, showing the LNWR-style signal box, which has since been removed. Dual-current unit No 313002 in Network SouthEast livery is en route to Watford. The hanging baskets of greenery beneath the canopy add a pleasant touch. *F. Hornby*

station, one leading to the booking office, the other, at the London end, linking with the high-level island platform of the North London line, which crosses at right-angles. There is a double-track electrified spur connecting the two lines, now little used but which once provided an alternative route for trains between Broad Street and Watford.

Beyond Willesden Junction the DC and main lines remain separated by freight yards and carriage sidings for a further 2 miles, the stations at Harlesden and Stonebridge Park being on this stretch. The DC tracks then burrow diagonally beneath the main lines, emerging on the down side and keeping parallel with them for another 8 miles. Several of the stations between Willesden New and Watford are still in the style dating from the opening of the New Lines in 1913, with two well-sheltered platforms and neat red-bricked buildings and retaining walls. One exception is Wembley Central, the first station after the lines have

As a welcome reminder that by no means all suburban stations are unstaffed and covered in graffiti, observe this splendidly maintained example at Hatch End. Built for the New Lines in 1911, its LNWR origin is proudly displayed beneath the decorative carvings. *F. Hornby*

changed sides, where a large raft of shops and offices covers the entire platform length and spans all the running lines – the result of a property development commenced in 1963 and costing £3 million.

There are four more stations in the next 3¼ miles, the second being South Kenton, opened on 3 July 1933 with an island platform to serve a populous area close to Northwick Park. The fourth is Harrow & Wealdstone, terminus for the Bakerloo Line trains, which reverse in a siding between the running lines at the Watford end of the station. The DC and Bakerloo trains connect here with the semi-fast Milton Keynes and Northampton services on the main line.

Carpenders Park, three stations beyond Harrow, was rebuilt in 1952 to a similar style to that of South Kenton to cater for nearby housing estates. in 1957 annual ticket sales here reached 1.3 million, plus over 32,000 season tickets!

Next comes Bushey, where the DC lines swing sharply away from the main line to make a wide loop through Watford High Street station after crossing the River Colne on a long viaduct, then returning to terminate alongside the main line at Watford Junction.

Between the viaduct and High Street station is the junction with the 1½-mile branch to Croxley Green, opened in 1912 and electrified in October 1922. The branch has two intermediate stations, the first of which was opened as recently as December 1982 for the sole benefit of the adjacent Watford Football

Club ground. Until January 1967 the same junction had also accessed a 3-mile branch westwards to Rickmansworth (Church Street). This had opened in October 1862, closely following the River Colne, with no intermediate stations, and lost its passenger service in March 1952. As laid, the junction was triangular, but when through trains between Croxley Green and Euston were discontinued, the east-west spur used by them was taken up.

Watford High Street station has an island platform with a sheltering canopy cantilevered between high retaining brick walls. It is well patronised, being much nearer the shopping centre than Watford Junction, where four terminal platforms are available for the DC trains.

On the Rickmansworth and Croxley Green branches the terminal stations were similar, with single platforms, neat buildings, run-round loops and sidings for goods traffic. Although the station at Croxley Green is still open – just – the station building was demolished in 1989. In earlier days the branches, being single track, offered the fairly rare experience of seeing the motorman 'collecting the tablet' at the junction.

Colour-light signalling on the DC lines between Camden and Watford dates back to 1933; Euston's rather archaic signalling was modernised in 1952 when an electrically operated box came into use. Thirteen years later, in conjunction with the rebuilding, it in turn was replaced, the new installation controlling the DC lines as far out as Queens Park as well as the main lines. A further advance came in January 1977 when Willesden Junction box took over from mechanical signal boxes between Queens Park and Stonebridge Park. Then in December 1988 a new power box at Willesden replaced the LNWR boxes at Willesden low level and Harrow & Wealdstone No 2, as well as two emergency ground frames – part of a £2.94 million project.

Fortunately serious accidents on the DC lines have been rare, and when mishaps have occurred the inconvenience has been minimised by the semi-fasts on the adjacent main lines making extra stops where platforms are available, at Queens Park, Wembley Central, Harrow & Wealdstone and Bushey.

Services

In 1948 the DC lines timetable showed little attempt to standardise departure times, the earliest Euston-Watford service being at 05.10 with two trains in the first hour, building up to four per hour in the morning peak, then fluctuating between two and four per hour until the last departure at 00.45. South Hampstead saw its first train at 06.14 and its last at 18.57, otherwise the majority of trains called at all 17 stations. The standard timing was 45 minutes for the 17¾ miles – a respectable 23½ miles per hour with stops on average only a mile apart.

It must be remembered that in those days there were also frequent trains between Broad Street and Watford, joining the line from Euston near Chalk Farm station (renamed Primrose Hill in 1950). The weekday tally was 63 departures from Euston and 34 from Broad Street, with 60 and 44 respectively on Saturdays when, of course, there were more trains around midday and fewer in the afternoon. On Sundays there were half-hourly trains all day in and out of Euston, but the Broad Street service was confined to the afternoon and evening, and indeed was withdrawn completely by the following year.

Both the Croxley Green and Rickmansworth branches saw more trains to and from Watford Junction on Saturdays than on weekdays,

doubtless with shoppers in mind; Croxley Green had 41 as against 29, while Rickmansworth had 34 as against 20. Neither branch had off-peak services on weekdays, where there was a six-hour gap from 10 am. On Sundays they both had hourly trains throughout the day.

The Rickmansworth branch was closed to passengers on 3 March 1952 and the Croxley Green service was gradually reduced – in 1953 it was down to 32 Saturday and 22 weekday trains – but there were no significant changes in the services between Watford and London at that time.

Moving on to the 1960s, the replacement of the LNWR EMUs by new Eastleigh-built units had made little difference to the journey times – just 1 minute had been shaved from the Euston-Watford schedule, but a 15-minute-interval service on this line from 7 am until midnight did represent an improvement. The 1966 timetable, as an example, listed 15 departures from Harrow & Wealdstone on the DC up line between 8 and 9 am – four each for Euston and Broad Street and three Bakerloo line trains for Elephant & Castle. By that year the weekday Croxley Green service had been further reduced, to 14 down and 12 up trains plus one each way to and from Broad Street. The branch survived closure proposals, although the through train was withdrawn, and weekday services were maintained throughout the 1970s. However, the Saturday trains ceased to run, shoppers having presumably taken to using their cars!

Economy measures introduced in 1976 resulted in the DC lines frequency being scaled down from 15 to 20 minutes on both the Euston and Broad Street services, with a 7-hour off-peak gap in the latter. During these hours, as on Sunday mornings, the Broad Street-Richmond trains provided a connection at Willesden Junction with those between Euston and Watford. It is noteworthy that one morning train from Watford to Broad Street was routed on to the North London line via the Willesden spur, rather than via Chalk Farm. In the 1985 summer timetable, a year prior to Broad Street's closure, there remained only five up and six down trains between the City terminus and Watford, all in the Monday to Friday peak hours.

The story of Broad Street's decline belongs more appropriately to the chapter dealing with the North London line, but after its closure in June 1986 the DC line stations to Watford suffered a marked reduction in their peak-hour services. By way of partial compensation for City workers, a limited number of trains commenced running between Watford and Liverpool Street from 30 June 1986, via a new curve at Graham Road linking the North London and Great Eastern lines. This service was, however, soon reduced, and ultimately discontinued from 25 September 1992.

In the 1993/94 timetable the Monday-Saturday regular interval service of three trains per hour between Euston and Watford was still operative, reduced to half-hourly on Sundays. The future for the Croxley Green branch, however, would seem bleak, as only one train each way survived, early on weekday mornings!

The Bakerloo tube trains continued to work through to and from Watford Junction until 24 September 1982, albeit confined to four trains each way at peak hours only from October 1965. To maintain this service four trains were stabled overnight in the BR depot at Croxley Green. Prior to their withdrawal, severe weather in early 1982, combined with intermittent ASLEF strikes, had caused dislocations from time to time until mid-July.

Thereafter no Bakerloo trains ventured northwards from Queens Park on to the DC lines until 4 June 1984, when a peak-hour service was restored as far as Harrow & Wealdstone. This was extended to operate all day Mondays-Saturdays from 16 May 1988 and on Sundays from 21 May 1989.

It is interesting to recall that in 1951, during the time of the Festival of Britain, Bakerloo trains connected with special excursions on Saturday mornings at Wembley Central, and ran non-stop through to Waterloo.

Traction and trains

As previously mentioned, the first LNWR electric trains were introduced in May 1914 for a Willesden Junction-Earls Court service, which, incidentally, ceased to operate in October 1940, its demise hastened by air raid damage. They were three-car units of centre-gangway saloons, comprising a Motor Brake 3rd, a Trailer and a Driving Trailer, with manually operated sliding doors, some cars being divided into 1st and 3rd Class saloons. The motor coaches had a switchgear compartment and luggage space behind the driver's cabin, the electrical equipment being supplied by Oerlikon of Switzerland. Current at 630V DC was collected from an outside conductor rail, with a centre fourth rail bonded to the running lines.

Units for the Euston and Broad Street services were built to this design in batches up to 1923, plus an accident replacement in 1926, and they earned the deserved reputation of being smooth-riding and comfortable. They soldiered on throughout the 1950s, the last survivors being used on the Croxley Green 'shuttle' in 1959.

They were joined in 1927 by three-car units of compartment stock of LMS design, formed of Motor 3rds, Composite Trailers and Control Trailer 3rds, seating 240 3rd Class and 40 1st Class passengers. They rode less well than their heavier LNWR predecessors, but the late Hamilton Ellis described the 1st Class as 'sumptuous'.

Both the LMS and LNWR trains were repainted after nationalisation from LMS maroon into the BR standard green livery for multiple units. During 1957 they were joined by the first of 57 three-car slam-door sets of Eastleigh design and construction, with a marked affinity to contemporary Southern Region 'EPB' stock, with two-digit headcodes but with shorter 57-foot frames and screw couplings. They weighed 106 tons, seating 252 in what was by then designated 2nd Class accommodation, and were powered by four GEC motors rated at 740 hp, with a maximum speed of 60 mph. As delivered they were in malachite green livery, but were repainted at Wolverton in Brunswick green before 'Rail Blue' was adopted in the late 1960s, and finally blue-grey with yellow ends from the early 1980s.

Although all based at Croxley Green depot,

Above An Oerlikon EMU of LNWR 1914 design in BR green livery leaves Euston for Watford in September 1956. By the time they were withdrawn in 1959 these solid and comfortable units had notched up over 40 years of service, remaining substantially as built to the end. *A. J. Pike*

Left Wembley Central is shown here on 4 March 1961 before the start of the development that covered most of the station area within the next few years. The Euston-bound train in green livery consists of two three-car units of 1927 vintage LMS-built compartment stock. *F. Hornby*

Left An Eastleigh-built three-car EMU occupies the single platform at Croxley Green on 24 July 1969, on one of the dozen or so shuttle services to and from Watford Junction. *J. M. Tolson*

LONDON COMMUTER LINES

they worked on both the Euston and Broad Street services and were fitted with three bars across each droplight, thanks to tight clearances in North London line tunnels. As delivered the centre trailers were compartment vehicles, but these were converted to open saloons during the 1970s. Ultimately classified 501 under the 'TOPS' scheme, they had a life of some 28 years, being phased out in 1985 when dual-current Class 313 units were transferred from the Eastern Region. Final withdrawal was delayed by a maintenance dispute, and in May 1985 all duties reverted to 501s for a short time, with the closure of Croxley Green depot deferred. The end came, however, on 30 September 1985, after which some were converted into two-car Sandite units, while others languished in Sudbury yard awaiting disposal.

During their time in service, Stonebridge Park power station, which had supplied current since LNWR days, was closed in July 1967, since when power has been taken from the National Grid. Also, from August 1970 the DC

lines were converted from fourth rail to third rail operation, with the centre rail removed, save on the section shared with Bakerloo trains.

The Class 313s, originally built in 1976 by BREL York for the Great Northern inner suburban services, are 103-ton three-car units seating 232 Standard Class passengers in open saloons. They have power-operated sliding doors, end gangways between coaches and are fitted with a public address system. Eight GEC traction motors deliver 880 hp with a maximum speed capability of 75 mph, which must be very rarely attained in normal service! They currently monopolise the Euston-Watford and North London line services, 18 units being based at Bletchley for these purposes. All are in Network SouthEast livery, embellished with the 'North London Lines' logo, replacing that of the 'Harlequin Line' bestowed in June 1988.

By way of variety, during a maintenance dispute in 1987 a DMU was loaned by Bletchley depot to help out on the DC lines, together with a Class 122 single diesel car, which filled in on the Croxley branch. On Cup

Class 313 EMU No 313006, seen at South Kenton heading for Euston on 7 July 1987, was outshopped from BREL York in 1976. South Kenton station opened in 1933 to serve adjacent housing developments, with an island platform accessed by a footbridge, now replaced by a subway. *F. Hornby*

A Bakerloo tube train of 1938 stock on an Elephant & Castle to Watford service hurries past South Kenton on 21 March 1956. These trains performed well for some 45 years until displaced by the 1972 Mk II stock. Through running by Underground trains to Watford ceased in September 1982, marking the end of a 65-year long era. *F. Hornby*

Final day in May 1988 a Southern Region 2EPB unit was a rare visitor, shuttling between Euston and Wembley Central. Much earlier, during 1956, while current was switched off for permanent way work, a steam-powered push-pull train plied between Wembley Central and Harrow over the DC tracks.

For many years from 1939 onwards the Bakerloo trains consisted of 1938 stock in seven-car formations, incorporating suitably modified trailers of 1927 design. In 1967 additional six-car trains were transferred on loan from the Piccadilly Line, and it was not until April 1977 that replacements in the shape of 1972 Mk II stock trains began to appear. During 1971-6 some 38 trains of 1938 stock had undergone a programme of 'extra heavy overhaul', but withdrawals commenced in 1981 and the last units were transferred to the Northern Line in 1985, where they completed 50 years of yeoman service.

In 1983 15 trains of 1959 stock were allocated to the Bakerloo Line, entering traffic on 28 February, supplemented by an additional train in 1984 when the peak-hour service to Harrow & Wealdstone was restored. They were returned to the Northern Line in 1988,

when more 1972 Mk II stock became available, since when the whole service has been worked by this type. Latterly their appearance has been much improved by the application of red-painted ends and doors, and a wide blue band along the lower sides of the carriages.

MAIN LINES
Euston-Bletchley and branches (Stanmore, St Albans Abbey, Dunstable and Aylesbury High Street)

Routes and infrastructure

In the Steam Age Euston, the outer suburban trains could be found at platforms 6, 7 or 8, half-hidden between the much longer ones for the more prestigious long-distance expresses. No 7 was in fact electrified for use by the DC trains if required, but all three were of adequate length for the seven or eight coaches that constituted the normal loads. In the more systematically planned modern station the 25kV electric multiple units arrive at and depart from Nos 8 and 11, flanking the DC line

Suburban lines from Euston:
main line from Euston to Bletchley and branches

Miles	Name	Opened	Closed	Notes
From Euston				
0	Euston	7/1837		
3¾	Queens Park	1879		
5½	Willesden Junction	9/1866	12/1962	
8¼	Wembley Central	1842		'Wembley for Sudbury' to 7/1948
11½	Harrow & Wealdstone	7/1837		'Harrow' to 5/1897
13½	Hatch End	8/1842		'For Pinner' to 6/1956
16	Bushey	1841		'Bushey & Oxhey'
17½	Watford Junction	7/1837		
21	Kings Langley	1909		'& Abbots Langley' to 5/1974
23	Apsley	1938		
24½	Hemel Hempstead	7/1837		Opened as 'Boxmoor'
28	Berkhamsted	1838		
31¾	Tring	10/1837		
36	Cheddington	1839		
40¼	Leighton Buzzard	7/1837		'Leighton' 1837-59
46¾	Bletchley	1838		
Stanmore branch				
	Harrow			
1	Belmont	9/1932	10/1964	'Halt' until 1934
2	Stanmore Village	12/1890	9/1952	'Stanmore' to 9/1950
St Albans branch				
	Watford Junction			
¾	Watford North	1910		
1¾	Garston (Herts)	2/1966		
3¼	Bricket Wood	1853		
4½	How Wood	10/1988		
5	Park Street	5/1858		'Park St & Frogmore' from 1890
6½	St Albans Abbey	5/1858		
Aylesbury branch				
	Cheddington			
2¾	Marston Gate	1860	2/1953	
7	Aylesbury	6/1839	2/1953	'High Street' from 9/1950
Dunstable branch				
	Leighton Buzzard			
4¼	Stanbridgeford	1849	7/1962	Private station until 1860
7¼	Dunstable	1848	4/1965	'North' from 9/1950

This 1953 photograph vividly recalls the old sprawling Euston, as BR Class '4' 2-6-4T No 80036 storms away from platform 7 with a stopping train for Tring. A Class '5' 4-6-0 in the background, also with 'stopping train' headlamp, awaits its turn for departure. Note the DC conductor rails in the tracks for platforms 4, 5 and 7. *A. J. Pike*

Only a few months after nationalisation, this pair of Stanier '4P' 2-6-4Ts, posed outside Watford shed on 26 March 1948, still bear testimony to their LMS origins. Ironically the site of this once busy little depot is now covered by a car park! *F. Hornby*

platforms, and sharing with them direct access for passengers to the Underground station. Stabling sidings for the EMUs are located outside the station on the up side, and on the down side at the top of Camden bank. This 1½-mile climb is no longer the hazard it was for departing steam trains, particularly in wet and slippery conditions when help from the engine that had brought in the stock was more than welcome.

Once clear of Camden the gradients out to Bletchley are far less severe, with a steady ascent to Tring at no more than 1 in 335 and an even gentler descent thereafter. This was achieved at the expense of heavy earthworks with long tunnels at Primrose Hill and north of Watford – the latter just over a mile in length – and a deep cutting at Tring. Much work and expense was therefore incurred when the line was later quadrupled to provide relief tracks for outer suburban and freight trains.

In earlier BR years there were five stations on the main line south of Watford, reduced to four when Willesden Junction (main line station) disappeared completely after closure on 3 December 1962. Of the remainder, Harrow & Wealdstone, then as now, was the most important. On 8 October 1952 it was the scene of one of Britain's worst rail disasters, in which an up local from Tring was one of the trains involved. There are platform faces here for all six tracks, those on the fast lines being little used. On the relief lines trains on the half-hourly Milton Keynes or Northampton services call throughout the day. Wembley Central, Hatch End and Bushey each had a sparse service in steam days – the latter still sees three trains each way at peak hours – while there are platforms at Queens Park for use in emergencies.

Watford Junction station was completely rebuilt during the 1980s, incorporating a curved platform for St Albans branch trains, built on a new alignment in 1984. There are two platforms on the old alignment, of which one is a terminal bay facing the London direction, while the track has been removed from the other. A car park occupies the site of the former six-road engine shed, for so many years home to a stud of suburban tank locomotives.

The seven stations between Watford and Bletchley, six of which date back to London & Birmingham days, are all still open but show few signs of their ancestry, having been suitably modernised. Some have seen considerable growth of the towns they serve, notably Hemel Hempstead, which currently has a population of around 80,000. Berkhamsted with 16,000 and Leighton Buzzard with 29,000 inhabitants have similarly expanded since the 1950s, but there is still much pleasant countryside along the line, which is closely paralleled from Kings Langley to Tring by the Grand Union Canal. Cheddington and Leighton Buzzard are no longer junctions, but the former had its day of notoriety as the venue for the 'Great Train Robbery' of 1963.

Although few main-line trains now start or terminate at Bletchley, it retains its importance as the junction for Bedford and as the maintenance centre for the outer suburban EMU fleet, with a depot and extensive sidings.

All the branches south of Bletchley save that from Watford to St Albans have closed since nationalisation. The nearest to London – and the shortest – was from Harrow & Wealdstone to Stanmore, just 2 miles long. Opened in 1890, it was single track, with a passing loop at the intermediate station at Belmont, and steeply graded, Stanmore being some 260 feet above sea level. The two stations differed greatly in style, reflecting the periods in which they were built. When the line was opened great pains were taken to ensure that the small single-platform terminus at Stanmore Village should blend with its surroundings; the building was strongly reminiscent of a country church,

complete with squat tower and ornamental spire. Belmont, opened in 1932, was far less ornate, with a booking office on trestles and a wooden footbridge leading to the island platform below. The passenger service was cut back to Belmont on 15 September 1952 and the branch closed completely in 1964.

The line from Watford Junction to St Albans Abbey dates from 1858 and is 6½ miles long with five intermediate stops. It is single track and was electrified at 25kV on 11 July 1988. The stations varied, from Bricket Wood, which originally had two fairly long platforms with a signal box on one of them, to the 'bus stop'-style halts. Abbey terminus had a roof spanning the island platform and one of the tracks, with run-round loops and sidings, and until 1951 was also host to two trains daily on an ER branch from Hatfield. It is now reduced to a single track and platform, while Bricket Wood has lost its loop, but at least the branch remains open, with a respectable service.

Both the branches north of Watford were rural in character. The oldest, from Cheddington to Aylesbury, 7 miles long with one intermediate station, opened in 1839 and was for many years the only railway serving the Buckinghamshire county town. The other branch, from Leighton Buzzard to Dunstable, followed in 1848 and was of similar length (7¼ miles), also with one station en route. End-on connection was made at Dunstable with a former LNER cross-country line from Hatfield via Luton. The branch was closed to all traffic in October 1967.

When describing the DC lines, mention was made of the way in which Euston's signalling system was modernised while the station was being rebuilt. Clearly such improvements benefited both suburban and inter-city traffic, and the 1965 box, on the west side of the station, had been preceded by a box at Watford, commissioned in July 1964, controlling from North Wembley to Cheddington and superseding 14 older boxes. A new form of track circuiting overcame the problem of interference arising from the proximity of DC and AC power supplies southwards from Watford. Willesden and Bletchley power boxes followed in mid-1965,

For 12 years after the closure of Stanmore in 1952, Belmont was the terminus of the short branch from Harrow & Wealdstone. This view in February 1961 shows the former island platform and the timber structure linking it to the booking office. Note that the passing loop has been lifted. *B. W. Brooksbank*

The answer to the question 'When is the next service?' could almost be 'Evensong', judging by the ecclesiastical appearance of Stanmore Village station, as seen in September 1951. Few London-bound commuters could have started their daily journeys in such attractive surroundings. *A. J. Pike*

controlling 13 and 33 track miles respectively and providing continuous modern colour-light signalling throughout – and well beyond – the suburban area.

On the Stanmore branch electric token block signalling had been installed in September 1938, with provision for either 'one engine in steam' or two-train working, with trains passing in the Belmont loop. This facility became superfluous when Stanmore closed and Belmont became the terminus.

Until removal of the Bricket Wood loop the St Albans branch was similarly worked in two sections of approximately 3 miles each. With only one train now in service at any time it is unsignalled save for automatic signals at Watford North, where a half-barrier level crossing is activated by the driver pressing a plunger.

Services

When the DC electric trains commenced running between Euston and Watford in 1922, they effectively removed all inner suburban traffic from the main line. As demonstrated by the accompanying table, the growth of towns beyond Watford, notably the conurbation centred on Milton Keynes, has warranted an expansion of longer-distance residential services, facilitated by the 25kV electrification that reached Euston in November 1965.

However, this was all some way into the future at the time of nationalisation, and in the 1948 timetable Bletchley, 46¾ miles out, was considered as the limit for outer suburban traffic. Weekday down trains terminated at Watford (two), Tring (five – including two

LONDON COMMUTER LINES

LM Region: Euston-Bletchley (46.75 miles) (Weekday down outer suburban trains)			
Year		1948	1994
Traction		Steam	25kV EMUs
To Bletchley	Total stopping trains	13	78
	Fastest time (mins)	80 (4 stops)	42 (2 stops)
	Average speed (mph)	35.05	66.8
	Slowest time (mins)	108 (12 stops)	57 (9 stops)
	Average speed (mph)	25.9	49.2
To Tring (31¾ miles)	Total stopping trains	18	51
	Fastest time (mins)	52 (3 stops)	34 (3 stops)
	Average speed (mph)	36.7	56.1
	Slowest time (mins)	76 (6 stops)	42 (6 stops)
	Average speed (mph)	25.0	45.35
To Watford (17½ miles)	Total stopping trains	23	83*
	Fastest time (mins)	25 (non-stop)	16 (non-stop)
	Average speed (mph)	42.0	66.6
	Slowest time (mins)	39 (3 stops)	23 (1 stop)
	Average speed (mph)	27.3	46.3

* 80 Mondays only

from Broad Street), Leighton Buzzard (one) and Bletchley (13). The latter were allowed as much as 108 minutes with 12 stops en route. There were, however, several additional fast trains with destinations further north, taking on average an hour to Bletchley with just one or two stops. Three trains ran 'all stations' from Watford to Bletchley, with connections at the former off the DC line. The Sunday service was sparse, with only seven departures from Euston – one each to Watford and Tring, and the remainder to Bletchley. It should be kept in mind that on weekdays there was far more freight traffic to share the relief lines than at the present time.

The Stanmore branch was favoured with a lavish shuttle service of 51 weekday trains (52 on Saturdays, none on Sundays) plus three early morning trips to and from the intermediate station at Belmont. The through journey time ranged from 5 to 7 minutes, the latter allowing for trains to pass at Belmont.

On the Watford to St Albans branch there were 24 trains each way on weekdays and Saturdays, plus an early morning working

between Watford Junction and Watford North. On Sundays there were 14 trains at hourly intervals. The journey time varied from 16 to 20 minutes according to operating needs.

North of Watford neither the Aylesbury nor the Dunstable branches contributed much in the way of commuter traffic. On the former, one train each way made London connections facilitating a through journey in just over 1½ hours, and on the latter just three down and four up trains made connections at Leighton Buzzard. The two branches lost their passenger services in 1953 and 1965 respectively.

By 1953 there was little discernible change in the main-line timetable, though there was a very slight improvement in journey times – the slowest train now reached Bletchley in 102 minutes! As to the branches, Stanmore had closed but there were still 36 daily trains shuttling over the 1 mile between Harrow and Belmont (40 on Saturdays), while the weekday service to St Albans Abbey had been enhanced to 27 trains. Patronage was increasing on this line, later rising in 1956 alone by 22 per cent.

With the introduction of the full main-line

Class AM10 unit No 070 on duty '2A04' calls at Harrow & Wealdstone on 6 August 1975 en route from Bletchley to Euston. Later classified 310, these 75 mph four-car EMUs inaugurated the 25kV outer suburban services in November 1965. *F. Hornby*

electric service on 1 March 1966 the basic off-peak timetable listed hourly trains between Euston and Bletchley taking 64 minutes with 10 stops – a respectable 43¾ mph – with another hourly train to and from Rugby via Northampton, making fewer stops and in most cases reaching Bletchley in 55 minutes at 51 mph. At peak periods the frequency was stepped up, with six departures from Euston between 17.00 and 18.00, three of which continued to Northampton or Rugby. All these were worked by the new AM10 multiple units.

Inevitably Bletchley has since been overshadowed by its near neighbour Milton Keynes, now served by half-hourly semi-fast trains to and from Euston. With a 65-minute schedule inclusive of 10 stops, the 46 mph average presents no problem to the Class 321/4 EMUs now in use. Other half-hourly trains go through alternately to Northampton and Birmingham, giving Watford and stations from Leighton Buzzard four trains per hour each way.

The Belmont branch had a frequent service right up to closure on 5 October 1964; Watford-St Albans could still boast 18 trains each way, plus a midday working as far as Bricket Wood, with 10 trains on Sundays. The line was, however, unprofitable, notwithstanding increased traffic, with a £24,000 deficit in 1965, so the branch stations became unstaffed halts to minimise losses. Nevertheless a new halt was opened at Garston on 7 February 1966 and – more recently – another at How Wood on 24

October 1988. Since electrification the service has been boosted to 26 trains each way on weekdays and Saturdays – mostly at 40-minute intervals – and 17 on Sundays, with a standard journey time of 16 minutes. The Sunday trains were withdrawn in October 1975 but, thanks to a subsidy from local councils, were reinstated two months later.

Traction and trains

During the war one could travel between Euston and Bletchley on a 'stopper' hauled by an ex-LNWR 'Prince of Wales' 4-6-0 from Bletchley shed, but these had gone by early BR days. By this time '4P' 2-6-4Ts of Fowler, Stanier and Fairburn design were the prime movers, though Stanier Class '5' 4-6-0s were not uncommon on the longer runs. On 30 July 1949 the author was impressed to find even more prestigious power on his up stopping train in the shape of 'Jubilee' 4-6-0 No 45653 *Bahamas*.

The 2-6-4Ts were distributed between the sheds at Willesden (three), Watford (12) and Bletchley (nine), hardly prolific when compared, for instance, with the 40 suburban tanks provided for the suburban services out of Marylebone. But there was no doubting their competence, and in 1949 *The Railway Observer* was able to report a run behind one of the Fowler engines with 300 tons, covering the 5¾ miles from Willesden Junction to Harrow in 8½ minutes start to stop. With

Above Under semaphore signals, Fairburn Class '4' 2-6-4T No 42150 arrives at Watford on 4 March 1961 with a semi-fast from Euston. All seven coaches are compartment stock of LMS 57-foot standard design. *F. Hornby*

Right During the interim between all-steam operation and the 25kV electrification, Derby-Sulzer Bo-Bo diesel-electrics replaced 2-6-4Ts and 4-6-0s on outer suburban duties. Here ML2 No D5143 (later Class 24) leaves Bletchley on an up train with the flyover to the Oxford line and a fine array of semaphores in the background. *F. Hornby*

relatively so few available it was inevitable that other locomotives were pressed into service; the same source recorded a Class '4' Ivatt 2-6-0 on an evening train to Watford in 1950, and a game performance in 1953 when little '2P' 2-6-2T No 41220 hurried its train from Euston to Watford in 25 minutes – well under schedule!

During the early 1950s BR Standard types made their debut; ten Class '4' 2-6-4Ts were allocated to Watford and four to Bletchley in 1952/3, joined at the latter by 10 Class '4' 4-6-0s. The BR 2-6-4Ts almost monopolised the shorter runs thereafter; when Euston, like Marylebone, was called upon to handle crowds of spectators for major events at Wembley Stadium with shuttle trains to and from Wembley Central, the 2-6-4Ts demonstrated their capabilities by taking loads of a dozen packed coaches in their stride.

'Super power' appeared on outer suburban trains in 1956 when the Southern Region 1-Co-Co-1 diesels Nos 10201-3 were operating on the LMR and filled in their diagrams on Bletchley locals, as did the LMS-designed Co-Cos Nos 10000-1. However, the eclipse of steam was still some years away, a start being made on 2 November 1959 when Derby-Sulzer 1,160 hp Bo-Bo diesel-electrics (later Class 24) took over some 2-6-4T turns. This was a gradual process, and unusual steam locomotives continued to enliven the scene, as for example in 1960 when Watford's '2P' 4-4-0 No 40672 made a rare appearance on an up stopping train.

Steam-hauled coaching stock consisted largely of 57-foot non-corridor compartment coaches, first introduced by the LMS in 1923 and built in batches for many years thereafter – wooden-bodied up to 1930, then with outer steel panelling, and from 1933 in a flush-sided version. Variations included nine-compartment 3rds, 1st/3rds, Brake 3rds and a few eight-compartment 1sts. As production continued until 1950 it is not surprising that they were still in evidence up to electrification. Older pre-grouping vehicles persisted well into the 1950s, low-roofed veterans of 'Midland' origin among them.

As the 25kV catenary came ever closer to London, steam shed closures came in quick succession; Watford closed on 29 March 1965 and Bletchley – to steam traction – in July of that year. The new AM10 EMUs (later Class 310), in royal blue livery, entered service from 22 November, working at first to the existing timings. These four-car units have a maximum speed of 75 mph and remained in service until early 1989, when they were gradually transferred away with the advent of their successors of Class 317.

Meanwhile, other classes appeared from time to time; in March 1975 a maintenance staff dispute resulted in cancellations and shorter trains and the substitution of a few of the older AM4 (Class 304) 800 hp four-car sets, normally based further north. In June 1980 a Class 312 unit, similar to the 310s but rated at 90 mph, helped alleviate a stock shortage, and in December of the same year, when the 310 units were experiencing problems with disc brakes, a Class 86/3 Bo-Bo electric locomotive with nine coaches gave commuters a taste of 'InterCity' comfort. The ASLEF dispute of 1982 saw 12-car formations of 310s for the first time, creating problems at intermediate stations with short platforms.

The Class 317 units of 1981 vintage, already familiar on the Midland division, were drafted to the services out of Euston from late 1987, and by March 1988 there were 20 based at Bletchley, increased by August to 35, which,

with the 18 remaining Class 310s, made up the depot's allocation of 53 units. Regular travellers pronounced them less comfortable than their predecessors but, thanks to a maximum speed of 90 mph, better timekeepers. The mix of two classes continued a little longer, with just two 310s still in peak-hour use in April 1989, but within a month yet another new class was destined to appear, which would in due course monopolise all the outer suburban duties.

The first unit of Class 321 (irreverently known as the 'Dusty Bins' thanks to a contemporary TV quiz show) emerged from BREL York in 1988, and in May 1989 a new batch – series 321/4 – was allocated to Bletchley. These four-car units are capable of 100 mph, and Bletchley's full complement of 42 units covers 38 daily diagrams.

Over the years the branches have seen as much motive power variety as the main line. Both the Harrow-Stanmore and Watford-St Albans branches were among the last preserves of ex-LNWR Webb '1P' 2-4-2Ts as late as 1948, though the regular engines were Fowler '3P' 2-6-2Ts and Stanier '2P' 0-4-4Ts, all based at Watford shed. Incidentally, the 0-4-4Ts were the first new class to appear during the Stanier regime and were no more than updates of a 50-year-old Midland Railway design.

On the Stanmore line the trains consisted of two-coach push-and-pull sets, with two trains in action at peak hours when as many as 100 passengers per set would be carried.

By 1951 the Ivatt '2P' 2-6-2Ts were also regular performers, and between 1952 and 1959 an experimental ACV diesel unit of three lightweight bus-bodied four-wheel vehicles was active in the area, firstly on the St Albans branch and from 1954 between Harrow and Belmont. Cracked frames caused problems in 1959, possibly to the relief of many travellers, as the unit had earned an unenviable reputation for rough riding. A BR Class '2' 2-6-2T on loan from Bletchley also did a stint on the Belmont 'shuttle' in March 1958. In later steam days a BR class '4' 2-6-4T was used on the Watford-St Albans line, somewhat disproportionate to its two-coach train, and a 'Derby lightweight' DMU in the M79XXX series with two 150 hp

EMU dimensions					
Class	Year introduced (builder)	Traction motors	Max speed (mph)	Weight per four-car unit (tons)	Seating (1st/2nd)
AM10/310	1965 (BR Derby)	4 x 270 hp EE	75	158.0	25/293
317	1981 (BR Derby/York)	4 x 332 hp GEC	90	137.4	22/269
321/4	1989 (BREL/York)	4 x 332 hp Brush	100	137.9	28/291

Right Arguably the Class 310 EMUs looked their best during the blue-grey period between the rather drab 'Rail Blue' and the garish NSE livery of the present day. Here No 310080 pauses at Watford on an up service on 2 March 1984. *F. Hornby*

Below Seen from South Kenton DC line station on 29 November 1989, a Class 321/4 EMU hurries past on the down slow en route to Milton Keynes. These units consist of two Driving Trailers, a Trailer and a Motor Coach (with pantograph). *F. Hornby*

Many a branch might possibly have been saved had BR persevered with such cost-effective alternatives as this experimental ACV bus-bodied diesel unit No 1. Consisting of three four-wheeled vehicles, it is seen at Watford Junction on 23 August 1952 when on trial on the St Albans branch. *F. Hornby*

engines was also a regular performer. Later on, diesel units of Classes 104, 105 and 108 played their part, in four-car multiples at busy times as traffic continued to grow.

The branch was electrified from 11 July 1988, with Class 313 units – working on 25kV power as a change from their usual 700V DC duties – in place of the diesels. They in turn were displaced by the superior Class 321/4 when sufficient units were available, though the 313s reappeared for a short while in the summer of 1990.

Motive power for the Aylesbury and Dunstable branches had been provided by Bletchley shed, Class '2P' 2-6-2Ts being the usual performers, but as a nice touch of nostalgia on the day that the Aylesbury branch closed to passengers (2 February 1953) Webb '1P' 2-4-2T No 46601 officiated, to the delight of the enthusiasts.

5.
LINES FROM ST PANCRAS

St Pancras/Moorgate/Blackfriars-Bedford
Kentish Town/Gospel Oak-East Ham and Barking

The Midland Railway came to Town from the north – setting an example followed by the Great Central 30 years later – and opened its own imposing terminus at St Pancras on 1 October 1868.

Completion of the 49¾-mile extension from Bedford put an end to the arrangement whereby, for the previous 10 years, the Midland had shared Great Northern metals from Hitchin into King's Cross. The high tolls charged by the GNR and growing congestion along the line created an intolerable situation, forcing the Midland to press ahead with its own right-of-way into London.

As with the other trunk lines to the north-west and west of the capital, suburban traffic was slow to develop, although six stations were provided in the first 4 miles from St Pancras, five of which eventually succumbed to tube and bus competition. Beyond the built-up area there were few places of consequence south of Bedford – even the cathedral city of St Albans was then of no great size. In early years most local trains served Moorgate rather than St Pancras, via tunnels from St Pauls Road Junction linking with the Metropolitan 'Widened Lines'. By the turn of the century, however, when communities such as Hendon were expanding, the tide turned in favour of St Pancras; in 1903 there were 38 local trains in and out daily, while Moorgate's share gradually declined. Some 80 years later history was to repeat itself with the introduction of the full electric service in July 1983, when Moorgate once again featured prominently in the timetable. Then, just five years later, with the inauguration of 'Thameslink', the great majority of suburban trains were re-routed via Blackfriars into Kent, Surrey and Sussex, even reaching the coast at Brighton!

The service from Kentish Town to East Ham and Barking resulted first from the opening of the Tottenham & Hampstead Junction Railway in 1868, then from its extension of 1894, the Tottenham & Forest Gate Railway, linking with the London, Tilbury & Southend at Woodgrange Park. The T&HJR became joint Midland and Great Eastern property in 1902 and thus LMS and LNER joint in 1923, while from nationalisation the boundary between the LMR and ER was located west of Crouch Hill.

Midland passenger services over the line commenced in October 1876, though not reaching the eastern extremities until 1894. The line was also used by Great Eastern trains between St Pancras and Cambridge, by Southend excursions until 1961 and by boat trains between St Pancras and Tilbury right up to 1963. In 1939 there were 19 trains from St Pancras and eight from Moorgate along the line, which also carried a heavy freight traffic.

When the Bedford-London extension opened, a class of 25 double-framed 0-4-4Ts of Kirtley's design was provided for local trains, replaced some years later by Johnson's slightly larger inside-framed variation. From 1907 onwards some ungainly 0-6-4Ts with 6-foot driving wheels appeared, but were unsuccessful and were banished elsewhere. During LMS years ex-L&Y and Caledonian types made brief appearances, but it was Fowler's 2-6-4Ts and 2-6-2Ts that supplanted the smaller Midland engines, and they continued to be so employed by BR until dieselisation.

Routes and infrastructure

St Pancras, notwithstanding its impressive roof with a single 240-foot span, is by no means one of London's largest termini, with only seven platforms. No 1 on the west side is the shortest, used exclusively for suburban trains, with Nos 2-4 also so used as and when required.

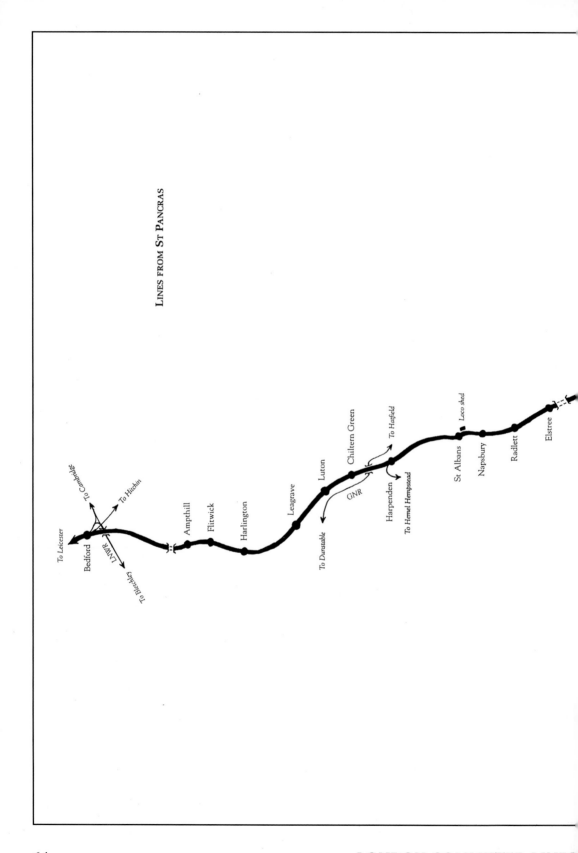

LINES FROM ST PANCRAS

LONDON COMMUTER LINES

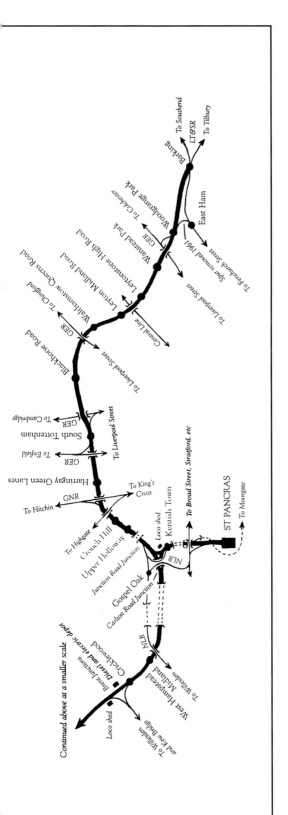

Continued above at a smaller scale

To Wildenden
and Kew Bridge

Loco shed

To Willesden

Cricklewood
Diesel and electric depot

West Hampstead
Midland

Brent Junctions

NLR

Gospel Oak
Carlton Road Junction

Junction Road Junction

Upper Holloway

Crouch Hill

To Highgate

Loco shed
Kentish Town

To King's Cross

To Hitchin

GNR

Harringay Green Lanes

To Enfield

GER

South Tottenham

To Cambridge

GER

To Liverpool Street

Blackhorse Road

GER

To Chingford

Walthamstow Queens Road

Leyton Midland Road

Leytonstone High Road

Wanstead Park

GER

To Colchester

To Liverpool Street

Central Line

Woodgrange Park

East Ham

Spur renewed 1961

To Fenchurch Street

Barking

LT&SR

To Southend

To Tilbury

ST PANCRAS

To Broad Street, Stratford, etc

To Moorgate

NLR

Ready for departure with a full head of steam, Fowler Class '4P' 2-6-4T No 42300 heads a local for St Albans at St Pancras on 15 February 1958. The first of a class of 125 locomotives, No 42300 was built at Derby in 1928 and was withdrawn in December 1960. F. Hornby

LINES FROM ST PANCRAS

65

Suburban lines from St Pancras, Blackfriars and Moorgate to Bedford, and Kentish Town/Gospel Oak to East Ham and Barking

Miles	Name	Opened	Closed	Notes
From Blackfriars				
	London Blackfriars	5/1988		
½	City Thameslink	5/1990		Opened as 'St Pauls Thameslink'
1¼	Farringdon	5/1988	'Thameslink' dates	
2¼	King's Cross Thameslink	5/1988		Opened as 'King's Cross Midland City'
	Moorgate, Aldersgate and Barbican	1865		
From St Pancras				
	St Pancras	10/1868		
1½	Kentish Town	7/1868		
4	West Hampstead Thameslink	1871		West Hampstead to 9/1950; West Hampstead Midland to 5/1988
5¼	Cricklewood	5/1870		Originally 'Child's Hill'
7	Hendon	7/1868		
9½	Mill Hill Broadway	7/1868		'Mill Hill' to 25/9/1950
12¼	Elstree & Boreham Wood	7/1868		'Elstree' to 5/1988
15¼	Radlett	7/1868		
18¼	Napsbury	6/1905	9/1959	
20	St Albans	7/1868		'St Albans City' to 5/1988
24¾	Harpenden	7/1868		'Central' from 9/1950
27¼	Chiltern Green	7/1868	4/1952	
30¼	Luton	7/1868		'Midland Road' from 9/1950
32¾	Leagrave	7/1868		
37¼	Harlington	7/1868		
40¼	Flitwick	5/1870		
41¾	Ampthill	7/1868	5/1959	
49¾	Bedford	2/1859		'Bedford Midland Rd' to 5/1988
From Kentish Town/Gospel Oak				
	Kentish Town	7/1868		
	Gospel Oak	5/1888		Present platform opened 5/1/1981
1½	Upper Holloway	7/1868		
2½	Crouch Hill	7/1868		
3¼	Harringay Green Lanes	1880		'Harringay Park' to 27/10/1958, then 'Harringay Stadium'
4½	South Tottenham	5/1871		
6	Blackhorse Road	7/1894		Resited 12/1981
6¾	Walthamstow Queens Road	7/1894		'Walthamstow' to 6/5/1958
7¾	Leyton Midland Road	7/1894		'Leyton' to 1/5/1949
8½	Leytonstone High Road	7/1894		'Leytonstone' to 1/5/1949

Miles	Name	Opened	Closed	Notes
9¾	Wanstead Park	7/1894		
10½	Woodgrange Park	7/1894		
11¾	East Ham	3/1858	9/1958	
13	Barking	3/1858		

Thanks to the whole station being well above street level – with what for many years were beer vaults below – no steep gradient is required to clear the Regent's Canal, which passes beneath the tracks a few hundred yards out, though cuttings and tunnels are much in evidence for the ensuing 3 miles.

At Kentish Town, 1½ miles out, the old locomotive shed has survived on the up side of the tracks, though no longer in railway use. The line to Barking diverged here via a triangular junction and spur, as well as once by a 'flyover', round to Junction Road Junction; only the west-north chord of the triangle survives and now sees little use. The main line turns west through Haverstock Hill Tunnel (1 m 73 yd), then north-west. Quadrupling took place many years ago in stages, necessitated by the heavy coal traffic rumbling south to Cricklewood. Additional freight lines from the yards there – now reduced to a handful of sidings – cross by a flyover to join the up and down slow lines at Silkstream Junction, north of Hendon. Hereabouts the railway crosses the River Brent on a 19-arch viaduct, with the M1 close by until road and rail part company where the latter plunges into the 1,050-yard-long Elstree tunnel. Beyond Elstree there are stretches of

In 1961, prior to extensive rebuilding, Kentish Town station still displayed evidence of its Midland Railway origins. A Bedford-bound Derby/Rolls-Royce diesel unit in the original green livery with 'whiskers' pauses at the down platform. *Lens of Sutton*

countryside even today, interrupted by Radlett and St Albans – now a thriving centre of 77,000 inhabitants – followed by Harpenden (pop 30,000) and Luton (165,000), a manufacturing town with a nearby airport.

Concurrently with dieselisation and electrification, all the intermediate stations were modernised with the loss of nearly all traces of the characteristic 'Midland' architecture, and a proposal to close St Pancras and divert the traffic into Euston and Moorgate was announced in 1967, but later reconsidered. The three stations remaining between Luton and Bedford were remodelled with platforms serving all four running lines, and a major rebuilding of St Albans City was completed in March 1973. Alterations took place at Luton in 1978 and a new station was opened at Bedford on 9 October of the same year. Normally stopping trains, with the few remaining freights, are confided to the 'slow' roads – something of a misnomer now they are passed for speeds of up to 90 mph!

Luton is the northern extremity of about one in three of today's 'Thameslink' services, and the 19½ miles thence to Bedford are quite thinly populated, although Flitwick has seen some development of late. There are no longer any branches with passenger services south of Bedford, and the only junctions are the former triangular one at Kentish Town with the Tottenham & Hampstead, and the surviving triangular one at Cricklewood with the line to Kew Bridge via Acton Wells Junction. A branch from Harpenden to Hemel Hempstead lost its sparse passenger service in June 1947, but remained open for freight traffic until 1964.

Gradients between St Pancras and Bedford, though undulating, are no steeper than 1 in 176, generally favouring southbound trains, with a summit of 323 feet above sea level at milepost 28¼ and a steady descent northwards from milepost 34 – certainly no serious impediment to modern traction.

The line from Kentish Town to Barking, 13 miles in length and double-tracked save for the last half-mile, forms a wide arc through Tottenham, Walthamstow and Leyton. At the east end the spur from Woodgrange Park to East Ham was closed in 1961, all trains having

Blackhorse Road station, on the Tottenham & Forest Gate section of the Kentish Town-Barking route, still displays solid and traditional architecture in this view looking west on 1 April 1961. An upper quadrant signal and the LMR 'lozenges' help to date the picture. *B. W. Brooksbank*

South Tottenham station is festooned with 25kV catenary between the junctions at either end and still boasts a well-kept signal box on the westbound platform. On 7 July 1993 Class 117 two-coach DMU No L413 departs en route from Gospel Oak to Barking. *F. Hornby*

been routed to and from Barking since 1958. At the west end the service was diverted from Kentish Town to Gospel Oak in January 1981, connecting there with the North London line. There are substantial engineering works along the way, with a mile-long tunnel between Junction Road Junction and Upper Holloway.

Much of the line is either in cuttings or on brick-arched viaducts, and crosses the reservoirs east of Tottenham by a causeway alongside the main road. Numerous other routes are crossed, including the main line from King's Cross and – until its closure – the Alexandra Palace branch. Further east, the lines from Liverpool Street to Enfield Town, Cambridge, Chingford and Colchester are crossed in that order, not forgetting the LT Central Line near Leytonstone; there are connecting spurs to all the BR lines save for the Chingford branch. The sections between the junctions at either end of South Tottenham station, and between Woodgrange Park and Barking, are now 'under the wires' for the much-reduced freight traffic; in early BR years there were over 30 freight trains daily in each direction. Recently there have been threats of closure and the intermediate stations have been reduced to 'basics', some of them unstaffed. In 1993 lengthy speed restrictions to 15-25 mph highlighted the arrears of maintenance work.

In a ceremony at Blackfriars on 25 April 1988, HRH The Princess Royal inaugurated the Thameslink service of through trains between the Midland and Southern lines. The north-south route across London is via the spur from St Pauls Road Junction to the Widened Lines, diverging at Farringdon and thence through the reopened Snow Hill Tunnel to Blackfriars, with gradients at the tunnel ends as steep as 1 in 32. Thereafter trains proceed via Elephant & Castle or London Bridge to their destinations in Kent, Surrey and Sussex. Farringdon is the changeover point between the overhead 25kV and third-rail 750V DC current supplies. King's Cross Thameslink station is rather inconveniently sited some distance from the main-line terminus, reached either via the street above ground or through the Underground station below.

Signalling on the main line, which was adequate in the 1940s for a 2-6-2T rattling along at 30 mph – when not checked by a freight in the section ahead – clearly would not suffice for EMUs capable of three times that speed. In 1948 lower and upper-quadrant semaphores were the order of the day, even at St Pancras where it was not until October 1957 that they were replaced by colour-lights, controlled from a new power box in place of three existing installations. The following year the tiny four-lever Tunnel box between St Pauls Road Junction and King's Cross (Metropolitan) was also closed.

In May 1965 all 50 route miles from Bedford to London were protected by AWS (Automatic Warning System), and the diesel multiple units were equipped with the appropriate receiving apparatus.

In preparation for electrification, work commenced in 1977 on a power signalling box at West Hampstead to control colour-lights and points over 70 route miles, replacing 29 old boxes. Resignalling was divided into seven stages, working from north to south, for completion in the autumn of 1981. In actuality the last mechanical box (Engine Shed Junction, at Kentish Town) closed in December 1981, and the final stage was completed with the closure of St Pancras power box in July 1982. Meanwhile track layout alterations resulted in the fast and slow lines exchanging functions for the first 1¾ miles out of the terminus, while further out the slow lines were suitably upgraded. Electric current was switched on into St Pancras on 27 September 1982, but the first public run in March 1983 was well behind schedule.

No such all-embracing modernisation has yet spread to the former Tottenham & Hampstead and Tottenham & Forest Gate line, along which several signal cabins still regulate train movements with a mixture of colour-light and semaphore signalling. Examples of the latter survive at the time of writing in the Crouch Hill-Harringay area, while at South Tottenham the junctions are controlled by colour-lights operated from a traditional-style box on the westbound platform. By way of architectural contrast the box west of Upper Holloway station is of wartime 'austerity' design. With the uncertainty hanging over the line, significant changes are unlikely in the foreseeable future.

Services

Table 218 of the London Midland Region 1948 timetable listed 16 stations between St Pancras and Bedford, three of which have since closed – Chiltern Green in 1952, then Napsbury and Ampthill in 1959. There were 31 weekday down stopping trains, of which details are shown in the accompanying table.

Additionally there were three trains from Moorgate – two to St Albans and one to Harpenden – and three short runs connecting with faster trains – one from St Albans to Luton and two from Luton to Bedford. Of the longer-distance trains from St Pancras, 11 stopped at Bedford, several of them calling at one or more intermediate stations; the fastest was non-stop to Bedford in 1 hour. Up trains closely replicated those out of London. The Saturday service was similar in total to that on weekdays, but on Sundays 12 stopping trains were deemed sufficient (five to Luton and seven to Bedford), plus nine fast trains, the up service being slightly better.

On the Kentish Town to Barking line there are ten stations averaging 1¼ miles apart, none having closed since nationalisation. Of 24 weekday eastbound trains 11 started from St Pancras and 13 from Kentish Town, four terminating at East Ham and the remainder at Barking. Journey time from St Pancras to either destination was on average 50 minutes, a somewhat sedate 17 mph! In the summer there were through trains to Southend, one of which started from Cricklewood – one could imagine a '4F' 0-6-0 enjoying a trip to the 'seaside'. A fairly good Sunday service of 15 trains, all to Barking, was supplemented by summer extras to Southend serving all stations along the line, including one from St Albans. All trains were '3rd Class only'.

Train service from St Pancras to Bedford, 1948								
From St Pancras to:								
				Slowest			Fastest	
	Distance (miles)	Trains terminating-	Time (mins)	Stops	Average (mph)	Time (mins)	Stops	Average (mph)
St Albans	20.0	7	55	7	21.8	34	1	35.3
Harpenden	24.75	6	66	9	22.5	40	1	37.1
Luton	30.25	7	78	10	23.25	47	1	39.55
Bedford	49.75	11	125	14	23.9	76	3	39.25

LONDON COMMUTER LINES

Seen from one of Barking's District Line platforms, Stanier '3P' 2-6-2T No 40167 and a three-coach train for Kentish Town occupy the terminal track on 11 October 1958. No 40167 was one of the six Stanier tanks rebuilt with a larger boiler, a modification which might well have benefited the rest of this rather underpowered class. *F. Hornby*

An apparently deserted Moorgate station is the setting for 'Bed-Pan' EMU No 317340, seen after arrival there on 5 May 1984. These 90 mph units revolutionised the Midland line service by comparison with their more staid diesel predecessors. *F. Hornby*

During the next decade main-line stopping services improved, more so as regards frequency than speed, with a regular-interval service off-peak. In 1959 there were 17 weekday trains to Bedford and 10 to Luton – both well up on 1948 – but it was the advent of the diesel multiple units that heralded a significant change. They first appeared on 28 September 1959 running to steam schedules, and a full-scale service commenced on 11 January 1960, but it was some time before teething troubles were eradicated. Thereafter the benefits were substantial, and introductory cheap day return fares helped ensure success for the new service. Patronage was quickly boosted by 20 per cent or more, and in due course St Albans alone was dispatching over 60,000 commuters to London every week.

The off-peak service from St Pancras consisted of an hourly train on the hour, all stations to Luton, and another fast to Elstree then all stations to Bedford. Journey time for the latter was 70 minutes with eight stops (42.6 mph), lopping 6 minutes off the steam schedule with only three stops. Moorgate passengers fared particularly well, with peak-hour trains non-stop between King's Cross (Underground) and Elstree, 16 minutes faster then their steam predecessors. The fastest times were in the up direction, for example, 21 minutes from St Albans and 26 from Harpenden, not far off 'even time'. These initial schedules must have proved slightly optimistic, however, as they were subsequently eased by 2 minutes or so.

As for frequency, Elstree was served by 45 daily trains instead of 30, St Albans by 100 instead of 79 and Luton by 88 instead of 50 – the two latter exclusive of long-distance

Mill Hill Broadway as portrayed on 19 May 1993 is typical of the 'modern age' suburban station with a minimum of shelter for northbound passengers. A pair of Class 319 EMUs forms a Luton-Sevenoaks train on 'Thameslink' service 'S1'. *F. Hornby*

expresses. At the same time diesel units took over on the Kentish Town-Barking line with an hourly off-peak frequency and some reduction in journey times, though there were complaints about poor connections at Kentish Town; just one up and two down trains served St Pancras with a running time of 38 minutes.

Subject to minor alterations, with the Moorgate service reduced to two trains each way prior to complete withdrawal in May 1979, the diesel service remained in operation for over 20 years until the Bedford-St Pancras section was electrified. On 17 May 1982, with much work in progress along the line, an emergency timetable was instigated, with some trains starting or terminating at Kentish Town. The first appearance of the new Class 317 electric multiple units at St Pancras was on 28 March 1983, and from 18 April they took over six daily runs, working to the DMU timings and restricted to 75 mph. The full service on what became popularly known as the 'Bed-Pan

line' was delayed due to protracted negotiations over 'one-man operation', and eventually commenced on 11 July 1983 with Moorgate once again playing a major role. Indeed, the basic timetable provided for half-hourly stopping trains from Moorgate to Luton and half-hourly semi-fasts from St Pancras to Bedford. Some of the additional peak-hour trains were non-stop to St Albans.

Inevitably there were problems to be ironed out before the service settled down – the power cars in particular proved to be rough riding – and EMUs of Classes 313 and 315 loaned from the Eastern Region together with Class 127 DMUs had to be substituted for a time. There could be no doubts, however, as to the vastly superior performance of the Class 317s with their 90 mph maximum speed; the standard timing from King's Cross (LT) to St Albans was 20 minutes for non-stops, as was that from St Albans into St Pancras. Even over so short a distance as from Harpenden to St

---

Train service from London to Bedford, winter 1993/94

From King's Cross (LT) to:	Distance (miles)	Trains terminating	Standard times and speeds		
			Time (mins)	Stops	Average (mph)
St Albans	20.25	5	30	7	40.5
Luton	30.5	35	45	9	47.33
Bedford	50.0	64	59	6	50.85

(Excludes trains from Moorgate)

Albans (4.8 miles) the maximum speed could be attained.

Relatively speaking, therefore, the next development, the launching of 'Thameslink' on 1 December 1987, heralded rather less spectacular improvements, albeit that the top speed of the new dual-voltage Class 319 EMUs is 100 mph. Even so, the north-south service represents a radical advance, although in reality reviving what was commonplace before the turn of the century, using the same reincarnated Snow Hill Tunnel. None of the weekday trains serves St Pancras, there being 29 northbound from Moorgate and a further 104 through the Snow Hill Tunnel to St Albans, Luton and Bedford. The accompanying analysis makes an interesting comparison with that for 1948.

Thus, inclusive of 29 trains from Moorgate, there are 133 trains as far as St Albans and over 100 thereafter – over four times as many as in 1948. On Sundays there is just one early morning stopping train out of St Pancras plus 36 through Snow Hill Tunnel. With the introduction of the full service on 16 May 1988 came the almost obligatory 'teething troubles', some failures being attributed to water seeping into the traction motors. These problems, combined with a massive upsurge in custom, resulted in overcrowding, but there is no doubting the popularity of the service, which could be further expanded but for the limited number of paths through the tunnel for a maximum of six trains each way per hour.

The long-standing link between the Midland line and Barking was severed when, from 5 January 1981, Kentish Town ceased to be the western terminus in favour of Gospel Oak. One of the last outposts of the 'Heritage' DMUs, the service frequency was reduced to hourly from 4 October 1993 and Sunday trains were withdrawn, running time being 34 minutes eastbound and 35 minutes westbound. Off-peak patronage is patchy, with the two-car units providing adequate capacity.

Traction and trains

Steam suburban motive power was based at Kentish Town (14B), where one of the three roundhouses was frequented by tank locomotives, at a two-road shed at St Albans (14C), and at Bedford (15D). At nationalisation Kentish Town and St Albans fielded between them some 15 Fowler and Stanier 2-6-4Ts, while Bedford maintained a stud of compound 4-4-0s for the semi-fasts, which were soon displaced by a further nine 2-6-4Ts. Additionally there was a fleet of some 36 '3P' 2-6-2Ts, mostly at Kentish Town and Cricklewood (14A), employed on the less demanding turns. Other classes occasionally seen on local passenger work included Kentish Town's brace of Ivatt '2P' 2-6-2Ts and even '3F' 0-6-0s on the short runs such as St Albans-Luton.

Early in the 1950s BR Standard classes displaced older engines. Kentish Town received four of the efficient 2-6-4Ts and Bedford five, together with Class '4' 4-6-0s Nos 75040-4 when new in 1953. These latter were transferred away for a while, but returned to displace the 2-6-4Ts in January 1955. Compound 4-4-0s from 'foreign' sheds made a brief reappearance in 1957, and the following year the less powerful '2P' 4-4-0s revived an old tradition by working Bedford semi-fasts. Just prior to dieselisation ex-LMS 2-6-4Ts gave commuters a thrill by working up to 80 mph with nine-coach trains, perhaps by way of a last fling!

Coaching stock consisted mainly of LMS-built 57-foot compartment vehicles, although flat-roofed carriages of Midland origin were not uncommon in earlier years.

On the Kentish Town-Barking and East Ham line the '3P' 2-6-2Ts held sway, though the Southend trains could produce a variety of more powerful locomotives. Similarly the Moorgate services were monopolised by 2-6-2Ts, in this case by the Fowler engines, which were condenser-fitted for working through the tunnels.

The author's own early Midland Division experiences included a lively run to St Albans in January 1949 behind '4P' Compound 4-4-0 No 41034 with six coaches, while by contrast '3P' 2-6-2T No 40112 made heavy going on the return trip with a stopping train of equal load. My first encounter with the 'Tottenham & Hampstead' was in May 1948 when a 2-6-2T –

The crew of Stanier '4P' 2-6-4T No 42453 appear eager for the 'right away' from St Albans with a Luton stopping train on 4 August 1958. The station has not yet been rebuilt and there are coal wagons in the sidings, now long gone. *F. Hornby*

Possibly one of St Albans's stud of 2-6-2Ts had failed on 17 August 1957, which would explain the unlikely presence of ex-MR '3F' 0-6-0 No 43565 on the 13.10 Harpenden-St Pancras stopping train. The elderly goods locomotive makes a clean getaway from Elstree with a lightweight rake, including a centre-gangway coach as 'swinger'. *F. Hornby*

Right 'Super power' for a Bedford-St Pancras stopping train, awaiting the road at Luton on 1 August 1959. Doubtless Fairburn 2-6-4T No 42133 is the rostered engine, while Class '5' 4-6-0 No 45274 is returning to London in the most convenient way after an unbalanced northbound run. *F. Hornby*

Middle right This scene was recorded at Elstree on 27 March 1954 and is typical of the period when BR Standard Class '4' 2-6-4Ts were much in evidence on the Midland Division. No 80060 of Bedford shed, half-shrouded in steam, heads a train of LMS-built 57-foot compartment stock. *B. W. Brooksbank*

Below Condenser-fitted Fowler Class '3P' 2-6-2T No 40022 scurries along near Radlett with a three-coach local on 30 August 1958. No 40022 was one of four such machines maintained at St Albans for less exacting turns, and became a casualty of dieselisation, being withdrawn at the end of 1962. *B. W. Brooksbank*

LINES FROM ST PANCRAS

At Luton on 1 August 1959 it is nearly the end of one era and the beginning of another. The brand-new Derby/Rolls-Royce diesel-hydraulic units are at the beginning of a 22-year tour of duty, while the sands of time are running out for 2-6-4Ts like the one at the far platform. *F. Hornby*

still with its LMS No 36 – handled a St Pancras to East Ham train of five ex-Midland Railway bogie coaches. I noticed that there were few passengers and that, even then, some stations looked 'unkempt'. In September 1951 a through train to Southend, calling at all stations, produced a '4F' 0-6-0 on nine well-filled coaches. The return trip was also on a through train, this time with a Fowler 2-6-4T in charge and badly delayed by a preceding freight.

Late 1959 saw the first of the Derby-built four-car diesel-hydraulic units appearing on the Bedford services. They weighed 139 tons, with four Rolls-Royce engines producing 952 hp and with a maximum speed of 70 mph. Later classified 127, they were of similar 'High Density' design to their Western Region contemporaries, with an all-2nd Class seating capacity of 352. Thirty units were allocated, but they were prone to breakdowns in the early stages, and substitutes ranged from the superannuated 2-6-2Ts to Class 2 diesel-electric locomotives. In the winter of 1961/62 the big

Class 4 'Peak' diesels lent a hand, and in the even more severe weather of 1962/63 steam made a brief comeback, with BR Class '5' 4-6-0s noted on stopping trains.

The Moorgate services were worked by Type 2 diesels with compartment stock, but a brief trial was made from 6 May 1968 with two-car Craven units, terminated abruptly after one caught fire near St Albans on 12 June. With these exceptions DMUs bore the brunt of the suburban services for 22 years, and in 1970 Cricklewood depot's allocation stood at 51 Motor and 66 Trailer cars forming Derby three- and four-car units. They were eventually phased out as the 'Bed-Pan' Class 317 EMUs came on stream in the early 1980s.

Details of these appeared in the preceding chapter on the lines out of Euston, to which they were transferred on the introduction of the 'Thameslink' service. Their stay on the Midland was thus relatively short, from their first appearance at Cricklewood depot in November 1981, and their first public run in March 1983, until the last two units left in August 1988.

'Thameslink' dual-voltage EMU No 319036, in Network SouthEast livery, rests in the sunshine at Luton on 11 August 1990 before its next foray through the tunnels into 'Southern' territory. With over 100 trains daily to and from London, Luton residents now enjoy a service four times that of 1948! *F. Hornby*

They were no less immune from the effects of Arctic conditions than their diesel predecessors and, in the heavy snow of 1984/85, only 20 of the full allocation of 48 units were available. This time inner-suburban Class 313 EMUs came to the rescue and – ironically – the withdrawal of the diesel units was deferred until the emergency was over!

History repeated itself when the Class 319 'Thameslink' EMUs made their debut in December 1987, as not only were there numerous failures, but, while on trial, they were 'blacked' when a cab footstep collapsed, injuring a driver. In consequence, in October 1989 some of the Class 317s reappeared on their old stamping-ground for a while, though not being dual-voltage-fitted they were not able to proceed beyond Moorgate. Problems besetting the 319s persisted throughout 1990, but with 86 units available in due course, the situation gradually improved. They consist of two Driving Trailer Standards, Motor Standard and a Trailer Standard, totalling 136.3 tonnes and seating 316. Maximum speed is 100 mph and each unit is powered by four 332 hp GEC motors.

The Kentish Town-Barking service, dieselised concurrently with that on the main line, was worked initially by four-car Class 127 units, subsequently reduced to three- and then two-car formations during 1983. In 1984 Birmingham RCW Class 104 units with 300 hp Leyland engines took over, and in 1986 Craven Class 105s from Stratford depot replaced the Cricklewood-based sets. To add to the variety the 'Crosstown Linkline', as it became known, has also seen Classes 101, 104 and even Class 121 single cars from Old Oak Common. These in turn gave way to Class 115s, made available from the Chiltern Line in February 1992 and which remain on the service at the time of writing.

6.
LINES FROM KING'S CROSS

King's Cross/Moorgate/Broad Street-Hitchin
Finsbury Park-Alexandra Palace
Wood Green-Stevenage via Hertford North
Branches from Hatfield (Hertford East, St Albans and Dunstable)

The Great Northern Railway's first London terminus opened at Maiden Lane on 7 August 1850 and was relocated at King's Cross from 14 October 1852, by which time four stations were open along the 17¼ miles to Hatfield. Three more had opened by 1861, and a service via spurs from either side of King's Cross station, through the tunnels and on to the Metropolitan to Farringdon Street, commenced in October 1863. This was extended across the river and over the London Chatham & Dover Railway into Victoria in July 1866, with trains provided by both the GNR and LCDR. To deal with this traffic the 'Widened Lines' were opened alongside the Metropolitan tracks in 1868.

Thereafter suburban traffic grew apace – on a far greater scale than on the lines to the north-west and west of London – with the building of the 'Northern Heights' branches from Finsbury Park to Edgware, High Barnet and Alexandra Palace. These, and the line from Wood Green to Enfield, opened in the 1860s and '70s. As with the Midland Railway a high proportion of the early suburban trains served the City, and in 1893 three times as many did so as used the main-line terminus. Finsbury Park became the focus of activity, eventually with five island platforms serving seven through tracks. In 1912 it dealt with 550 trains daily, including many operated by the North London Railway to and from Broad Street via a spur from Canonbury. This practice dated back to 1875 and was perpetuated by the LMS (still using four-wheeled carriages well into the 1930s!), and in BR days by the Eastern Region.

The first GNR engines built for the London suburban traffic were Sturrock's 0-4-2 well tanks of 1865, condenser-fitted for working over the Widened Lines, and these were followed successively by 0-4-4Ts, 4-4-2Ts and 0-6-2Ts of Stirling and Ivatt designs. The latter also introduced a class of massive 0-8-2Ts, which, less than successful, were banished to the north.

Some inroads were made into this intensive traffic as early as 1904 when the Great Northern & City tube line, built to main-line dimensions, was opened as a more direct route between Finsbury Park and Moorgate. It was never linked with the main system as intended, but nevertheless the GNR, and subsequently LNER, steam service to and from the City was much reduced outside peak hours. As laid the GN&C line had negative and positive conductor rails outside the running rails, but in 1939, when the original vehicles were replaced by smaller 'tube' stock, the current supply was converted to London Transport's standard fourth-rail system.

Because of the bottlenecks and congestion caused by the tunnels outside King's Cross it was realised that the 'Northern Heights' traffic could be more expeditiously handled by extending London Transport's Northern Line from Highgate Archway through East Finchley and thence over the LNER tracks to High Barnet. This project was completed in April 1940, and the Edgware branch was so treated as far as Mill Hill East in May 1941. Work then ceased due to wartime pressures, and the Alexandra Palace branch continued to be steam operated until closure in 1954.

The tube service on the High Barnet line was far more frequent than in steam days and boosted originating journeys from 3.5 to 12 million in a year. Thus the volume of traffic inherited by BR in 1948, though by no means insignificant, was considerably less than in the pre-war years.

Routes and infrastructure

By virtue of gradients and bottlenecks, the steam-worked suburban services on the Great Northern section were as difficult to operate as any in the London area, and the infrastructure in 1948 was little changed from that which had come into LNER ownership 25 years previously.

King's Cross station layout and its approaches were remodelled and simplified early in 1977, prior to which time there were five suburban terminal platforms, Nos 11-15 (renumbered 9-13 from 1972) on the west side of the station, all

---

Suburban lines from King's Cross/Moorgate to Hitchin (main line) and branches

Miles	Name	Opened	Closed	Notes
From King's Cross				
	King's Cross	10/1852		Terminus at Maiden Lane 8/1850-10/1852
2½	Finsbury Park	7/1861		'Seven Sisters Road' to 1869
	Finsbury Park-Canonbury spur opened for passenger services 1/1875; ceased 1976			
3½	Harringay	1885		'Harringay West' from 5/1950
4	Hornsey	8/1850		
5	Alexandra Palace	1859		'Wood Green' to 3/1971; 'Wood Green (Alexandra Palace)' 3/1971-5/1982
6½	New Southgate	8/1850		'& Friern Barnet' to 3/1871
8½	Oakleigh Park	1873		
9¼	New Barnet	8/1850		
10¼	Hadley Wood	1885		
12¾	Potters Bar	8/1850		
14½	Brookmans Park	1926		
15½	Welham Green	9/1986		
17¾	Hatfield	8/1850		
22	Welwyn North	8/1850		'Welwyn' to 7/1926
25	Knebworth	2/1884		
27½	Stevenage	8/1850		Original closed 7/1973; new opened 9/1973
31¼	Hitchin	8/1850		
'Widened lines'				
	Moorgate	2/1868		Opening date for GN trains
½	Aldersgate & Barbican	1865		
¾	Farringdon Street	1865		
1½	King's Cross York Road	6/1866	3/1977	
Former Great Northern & City line				
	Moorgate			
½	Old Street	1904		
1¼	Essex Road	1904		'Canonbury & Essex Road' to 7/48
2¼	Highbury & Islington	1904		
2¾	Drayton Park	1904		*Table continued overleaf*

Miles	Name	Opened	Closed	Notes
Alexandra Palace branch				
	Finsbury Park			
¾	Stroud Green	4/1881		
1¼	Crouch End	8/1867		
2¼	Highgate	8/1867	7/1954	
3	Cranley Gardens	8/1902		
3¾	Muswell Hill	5/1873		
4¼	Alexandra Palace	5/1873		
Hertford loop				
	Moorgate			
6¾	Bowes Park	1871		
7¾	Palmers Green	1871		'& Southgate' to 3/1971
8¾	Winchmore Hill	1871		
9½	Grange Park	4/1910		
10¼	Enfield Chase	4/1910		Replacing Enfield, opened 1871
11	Gordon Hill	4/1910		
12½	Crews Hill	4/1910		
14¼	Cuffley	4/1910		
17¾	Bayford	6/1924		
19¾	Hertford North	6/1924		Original station opened 3/1858, closed 6/1924
25	Watton-at-Stone	6/1924		Closed 9/1939, re-opened 5/1982
St Albans branch				
	Hatfield			
2	Nast Hyde Halt	1910		
2¾	Smallford (for Colney Heath)	11/1866		
4	Hill End	1899	10/1951	
5¾	St Albans London Road	11/1866		
6½	St Albans (Abbey)	5/1858		Opened by LNWR; closure date for ER service
Dunstable branch				
	Hatfield			
4½	Ayot	1877	1949	Destroyed by fire
7¼	Wheathampstead	1860		
9½	Harpenden East	1860		
12	Luton Hoo	1860	4/1965	
15	Luton (Bute Street)	1858		
19¼	Dunstable Town	1860		
20¼	Dunstable North	1866		Joint with LMR
Hertford North branch				
	Hatfield			
4	Cole Green	3/1858	6/1951	
5½	Hertingfordbury	3/1858	6/1951	
6½	Hertford North	3/1858		

A Craven two-car diesel unit pauses at King's Cross (York Road) platform on 27 February 1976 on a Welwyn Garden City-Moorgate service. This route was abandoned in November of that year when the inner suburban electrified service commenced, using the old Great Northern & City route via Highbury. *F. Hornby*

Although the 'Northern Heights' lines passed from LNER into London Transport hands as long ago as 1940, it is pleasing to see how the stations have retained their Steam Age character. In this view at Totteridge on 27 March 1985 a train of Northern Line 1959 stock is about to leave for High Barnet. *F. Hornby*

long enough to accommodate eight coaches with a tank locomotive at either end. Additionally No 16 (renumbered 14 from 1972) was a through platform on a 1 in 37 gradient for trains emerging from the Widened Lines via the notorious 7½-chain-radius 'Hotel Curve'. An unnumbered platform on the opposite side of the station, accessible from York Road, served their City-bound counterparts. All these platforms were closed on Sundays when local trains used the main-line platforms, as did some outer-suburbans at peak times during the week. The two through platforms became redundant when the electrified line from Moorgate to Finsbury Park became operational in November 1976, and from the following year, with the elimination of locomotive-hauled trains, two terminal platforms, Nos 9 and 10, were deemed sufficient. Later, as traffic increased, a third, No 11, was reinstated in October 1988. The

suburban platforms are little more than a road's width away from St Pancras, and thus both King's Cross and St Pancras share a common Underground station served by the Northern, Victoria, Piccadilly, Metropolitan and Circle lines. The sub-surface 'Thameslink' station is also close by.

Trains leaving King's Cross are faced immediately with a 1½-mile climb at 1 in 107, much of it in tunnels, with a further 8 miles at 1 in 200 from Alexandra Palace (formerly Wood Green). After the summit at Potters Bar there are undulations varying from 1 in 200 to 1 in 300 thence to Hitchin. Until 1959 there were two bottlenecks south of Stevenage caused by tunnels through which the suburban trains had to share two tracks with all other traffic. The first extended from Greenwood signal box, 10 miles out, for 2¾ miles through three tunnels to Potters Bar.

To Royston and Cambridge

To Peterborough

To Bedford

MR

Hitchin

Loco shed

Stevenage

Langley Junction

Knebworth

Welwyn North

Ayot

Watton-at-Stone

Hertford North

Hertford East

GER

To Broxbourne

Hertingfordbury

Bayford

Ponsbourne Tunnel

Cuffley

Crews Hill

Cole Green

Hatfield

Welwyn Garden City

Nast Hyde Halt

Welham Green

Smallford

Loco shed

Brookmans Park

Potters Bar

Harpenden

Wheathampstead

Hill End

St Albans Abbey

To St Pancras

MR

LNWR

To Watford

To Bedford

Luton
Bute Street

Luton Hoo

Dunstable

LNWR

To Leighton Buzzard

Alexand

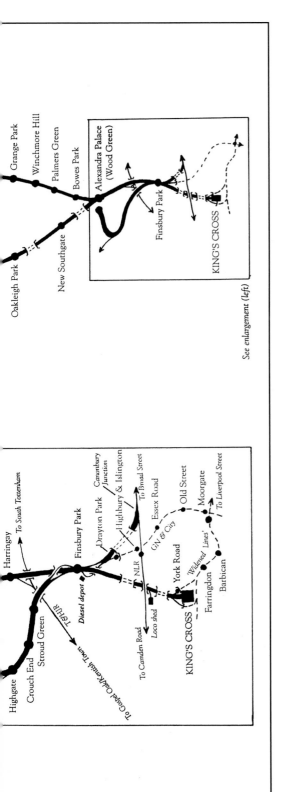

Grange Park
Winchmore Hill
Palmers Green
Bowes Park

Alexandra Palace
(Wood Green)

Oakleigh Park

New Southgate

Finsbury Park

KING'S CROSS

See enlargement (left)

Harringay

To South Tottenham

Finsbury Park

Drayton Park

Canonbury Junction

Highbury & Islington

To Broad Street

Essex Road

GN & City

Old Street

Moorgate

To Liverpool Street

Highgate

Crouch End

Stroud Green

T&HJR

To Gospel Oak/Kentish Town

Diesel depot

NLR

To Camden Road

Loco shed

York Road

'Widened Lines'

KING'S CROSS

Farringdon

Barbican

A peaceful scene in King's Cross suburban station on 11 May 1974 with a pair of Class 105 Craven two-car DMUs in 'Rail Blue' resting between duties. At this stage only two terminal platforms were deemed necessary as compared with five formerly. *F. Hornby*

Above Hatfield shed, though small, played a vital role in providing motive power for main-line and branch-line local passenger traffic with an allocation of some 25 0-6-2Ts. The station is just visible on the right in this view looking north on 23 May 1959. *F. Hornby*

Left The 1973-built station at Stevenage is one of the busiest in the Great Northern suburban area, served by long-distance expresses as well as by stopping trains via the main line and Hertford loop. A 90 mph EMU, No 317363, awaits the road before leaving for King's Cross on 29 July 1988. *F. Hornby*

Left Considerable realignment of tracks and rebuilding of stations preceded the suburban electrification of November 1976. Three-car EMU No 313034 is seen here pausing at a modernised Hornsey, en route to Moorgate on 4 February 1977. *F. Hornby*

This was eliminated by extensive engineering works commenced in 1955 and completed four years later. The second, extending for just over 2 miles across the 500-yard Digswell Viaduct and through two short tunnels to Woolmer Green, remains with us to this day. The removal of the first gives 21 miles of continuous four tracks from King's Cross, with the slow lines flanking the fast pair; this arrangement is resumed northwards from Woolmer Green.

Most suburban stations on the main line, save those in the bottlenecks, consisted of two island platforms serving all four running lines, but there were exceptions to the rule and the five 'islands' at Finsbury Park have already been mentioned; these have now been reduced to three, serving five tracks. Hatfield has staggered platforms with an island for down trains and a single platform on the up side. In the course of modernising, the tracks were realigned and a bay platform on the up side was removed, as were the sidings and engine shed. Hadley Wood and Potters Bar were rebuilt during the widening operations to conform to the 'two islands' pattern, and more recently a new station has been opened at Welham Green, 2½ miles south of Hatfield, with local line platforms only. This brings the number of stations on the main line between King's Cross and Hitchin to 16 in the 32 miles.

At Welwyn Garden City the station entrance is now incorporated in a shipping mall completed in October 1990. A flyover was provided south of the station in 1975 to facilitate the reversal of electric trains terminating there. Drastic measures were needed at Stevenage due to the dramatic expansion of the New Town – the population has grown from 6,000 to 75,000 in three decades – and the old station has been replaced by a new one a mile to the south with two long island platforms, opened in 1973. Hitchin, with platforms for the slow lines only – lengthened in 1989 – retains something of its pre-BR atmosphere, save of course for the disappearance of the adjacent locomotive shed and sidings.

Closer to London, Harringay and Hornsey were modernised with the loss of their main-line platforms and with the local tracks realigned preparatory for the suburban electrification of 1976, while Wood Green (since renamed Alexandra Palace) was updated in 1973, losing its gas lighting in the process!

The Alexandra Palace branch, having narrowly escaped incorporation into London Transport, continued to function spasmodically until final closure on 5 July 1954. As far as Park Junction, beyond Highgate, the route had been shared with the other 'Northern Heights' services to High Barnet and Edgware until 1940. Beyond this junction there were two more stations in the remaining 1¾ miles to the terminus. The station there, 310 feet above sea level, consisted of a wide island platform overshadowed by the Palace, which had attracted great crowds in

Two compartment coaches suffice for this off-peak train at Alexandra Palace on 6 March 1954. 'N2' 0-6-2T No 69519 is about to leave bunker-first for Finsbury Park, doubtless enjoying the respite from its more onerous main-line duties. *N. L. Browne*

earlier years; latterly the trains were almost deserted outside peak hours. The maximum gradient was 1 in 80, with tunnels at either end of Highgate station and with a 17-arch viaduct between Cranley Gardens and Muswell Hill. In its declining years it was hard to imagine that, years before, there had been through services to and from Victoria and Woolwich.

The present Alexandra Palace is the junction for the 24-mile loop line to Langley Junction, south of Stevenage, double track throughout and accessed by flying junctions at both ends. It opened in stages between 1871 and 1924, Hertford North being the terminus for suburban services for many years. There was once a connection to Hertford East on the GE section, though not used by passenger services; it was severed in October 1965.

When the loop was completed it formed a valuable diversionary route at times when the main line was blocked, although various restrictions limited the maximum speed along it to 50 mph. Engineering work involving single-line working at peak hours and off-peak bus

substitutions enabled the limit to be raised to 70 mph by the summer of 1960. Most stations have the conventional two platforms, though the southernmost one, Bowes Park, has an island platform, and in steam days Hertford North – then also the terminus of a branch from Hatfield – had two of them. There are two tunnels of which Ponsbourne, between Cuffley and Bayford, is 1 m 924 yd long. The northern portal marks the summit of a 7-mile climb followed by a steeper (1 in 198) descent to the second, short tunnel just beyond Hertford North. There are currently 11 intermediate stations, and traffic has greatly increased since electrification, although beyond Enfield the only town of consequence is Hertford, with a population of 22,000 and with another station served from Liverpool Street.

All the branches from Hatfield were cross-country lines terminating at places with more direct routes from London. The St Albans branch (1866-1951) was 6½ miles long with four intermediate stations; it shared St Albans Abbey station with the ex-LMS line from

On 14 May 1960, in the early months of dieselised suburban services, three Craven two-car units form a King's Cross-bound stopping train at Harringay. Note the flyover spanning the main line and the impressive array of semaphore signals. *F. Hornby*

Watford. The Hertford North branch (1858-1951) was of identical length but with only two stations en route. The longest branch, via Luton to Dunstable, was of 1860 vintage with six stations along its 20¼ miles and made an end-on connection with another ex-LMS branch, from Leighton Buzzard. It lasted into the diesel era, closing in April 1965. Though practically all trains on the Hertford and Dunstable branches worked through from and to Hatfield, they diverged from the main line, to the east and the west respectively, one station north at Welwyn Garden City. Between those two stations there was a single track for the Dunstable trains, on the down side of the main lines.

The conversion of the former Great Northern & City tube into a BR electrified line from Moorgate to Finsbury Park in 1976 enabled the old route via the Widened Lines to be abandoned. The line surfaces at Drayton Park, whence the down track burrows beneath the main lines from King's Cross. There is cross-platform connection with the Victoria Line at Highbury, with further access to the latter, and to the Piccadilly Line, at Finsbury Park. Coincidental with the closure of the old route, the peak-hour service to and from Broad Street via the Finsbury Park-Canonbury spur was also discontinued; the spur remains open for freight traffic.

The replacement of steam by diesel traction from 1959 onward and electrification some 17 years later enabled a more intensive service to be worked over a greatly simplified track layout, which in turn depended on a modernised signalling system. As of 1948 only the short section from King's Cross to Belle Isle was controlled by colour-lights, dating from 1932. Elsewhere upper quadrant semaphore signals were in vogue, with even a few somersault signals of GNR origin; a gantry of them at Finsbury Park was replaced by colour-lights in 1950.

Further out, save for a few distant signals, colour-lights were confined to the 3½ miles from New Barnet to Potters Bar, installed during the widening works. In 1970 approval was given to re-equip the main line and the Hertford loop, and work proceeded in stages

until April 1977, when King's Cross power box, controlling 830 trains daily, replaced 57 manual boxes. The slow lines were equipped with three-aspect colour-lights, save at the southern end of the Hertford loop where the close proximity of stations necessitated four-aspect signals.

In conjunction with track alterations the flyover at Holloway was upgraded from 15 to 30 mph for use by inbound suburban trains crossing from the east to west side of the main lines. At the same time the hitherto 'slow' lines were passed for 75 mph instead of 50 mph maximum speeds. For outer suburban trains using the fast tracks the permissible maximum rose to 100 mph beyond Alexandra Palace! A public address system was installed in the power box to relay information to passengers at any of 35 suburban stations, although 'regulars' would claim that the information was not always infallible!

Services

In the first years of BR's stewardship the rather complex GN line suburban services were virtually unchanged from those operated post-war by the LNER, with trains between Moorgate, Broad Street, King's Cross, Finsbury Park and a variety of stations on the main line and Hertford loop.

Exclusive of the Cambridge buffet car expresses, which called at Hitchin (and in most cases at Welwyn Garden City), the 1949 winter timetable listed 100 weekday suburban departures with destinations as shown in the upper table opposite.

These were spread over a long day; the first departure from King's Cross (Mondays excepted) was at 1.00 am and the last at 12 midnight. Typical journey times are shown in the second table.

There were 50 departures on Sundays – all from King's Cross save for two from Finsbury Park to Hertford North. These included some distinctly leisurely timings – for example, 81 minutes to Hitchin with 15 stops. The favourite Sunday destinations were Hertford North, Hatfield and Welwyn Garden City. On summer Saturdays, incidentally, all suburban trains

Hertford North no longer needs a water tank, and the semaphore signals are long gone since this scene was recorded on 20 September 1958. The fireman is clambering down from the bunker before 'N2' 0-6-2T No 69572 leaves with the 1.31 pm to King's Cross. *F. Hornby*

were routed to Moorgate to ease the strain on an over-taxed King's Cross. The Broad Street services, inherited from the LMS, were worked after nationalisation by ER locomotives and stock and confined to peak hours.

As reported in the contemporary *Railway Observer*, the 5.34 pm departure from Moorgate made post-war history by being scheduled to run through King's Cross without stopping, on an 11-minute 'sprint' from Farringdon Street to Finsbury Park, where it was then one of three northbound trains leaving within 2 minutes!

The Alexandra Palace branch was well served by 24 'weekdays only' trains from Finsbury Park, of which all but two made good

GN line down suburban services, 1949

From:		King's Cross	Finsbury Park	Moorgate	Broad Street	Total
To:	Gordon Hill	3	4	-	2	9
	Cuffley	-	-	1	1	2
	Hertford North	19	6	5	3	33
	New Barnet	2	1	2	1	6
	Potters Bar	-	-	1	-	1
	Hatfield	7	-	2	-	9
	Welwyn Garden City	9	1	1	1	12
	Hitchin and beyond*	28	-	-	-	28
	Total	68	12	12	8	100

* Mostly Baldock or Royston

GN line suburban train timings, 1949

	Distance (miles)	Stops	Time (mins)	Average (mph)
King's Cross-Hertford North	19¾	13	57	20¾
King's Cross-Hitchin	31¾	8	72	26¼
Moorgate-New Barnet	10¾	6	36	18
Broad Street-Gordon Hill	12¼	9	44	16¾

connections from King's Cross. The first morning train terminated at Highgate, the remainder running through to the Palace in 17 minutes for the 4¾ miles inclusive of six stops; this 17 mph average reflected the steep gradients and short distances between stations.

The service on all three branches from Hatfield was sparse. However, save for the first train of the day to Hertford North, all the others made connections to or from King's Cross, and a through train from Luton is worthy of note.

In 1951 service cuts gave rise to many complaints, as is not surprising when – to quote an extreme example – there was no train from King's Cross to New Barnet, a mere 9 miles away, between 6.59 pm and 9.21 pm. The Alexandra Palace service was withdrawn on 27 October but, with most of the cancelled trains on the main line, was restored on 7 January 1952. The Hatfield to Hertford North branch lost its passenger service -permanently – on 14 June 1951, followed in October by closure of the St Albans branch. Workmen's tickets, as on other lines, were replaced after 30 September 1950 by early morning returns.

By 1953 marginal improvements were made in the main-line and Hertford North stopping services, though journey times were unchanged. At least the residents of New Barnet now had two trains in the evening between 7 and 9 pm! The Alexandra Palace branch saw its last trains on 5 July 1954 after an eventful existence of 81 years.

It was not until late 1958, however, that significant changes were implemented, thanks to the completion of the widening works at Potters Bar and the introduction of diesel traction. The last 'all steam' timetable was that for Summer 1958, though a considerable period elapsed before steam was finally ousted, but by the early 1960s the advantages of the new motive power were becoming evident. In Summer 1961 there were 130 weekday stopping trains arriving in London, including 73 designated for diesel traction, from 13 points of origin. The accompanying table shows that diversity was still high. Journey times showed improvements ranging from 19 minutes (Hitchin-King's Cross) to 5 minutes (Gordon Hill-Broad Street).

Services along the sole remaining branch, between Dunstable and Hatfield, were little changed from 1949, still with the Luton-Dunstable short workings and a through train from Luton to King's Cross.

There followed a period of relative stability while diesel traction was consolidated, one innovation being the restoration on 5 March 1962 of services between Hertford North and Hitchin – worked pre-war by a Sentinel railcar but now by a diesel unit – with seven trains each way daily.

During the 1960s the off-peak timetable listed two stopping trains per hour between King's Cross and Hertford North, one between King's Cross and Welwyn Garden City, omitting some stops, and one between Finsbury Park and Hatfield or Welwyn Garden City. The other suburban customers were catered for by an hourly train between King's Cross and either Baldock or Royston, non-stop south of Hatfield. Cambridge had an (approximately) hourly service, also fast south of Hatfield or Welwyn Garden City. Enforced economies resulted in some highly unpopular cuts in evening peak-hour services in October 1971.

Electrification came later in the 1970s in two stages, the first covering the inner suburban services from Moorgate over the former GN & City line, thence to Hertford North and Welwyn Garden City; good connections with the diesel outer-suburbans were provided at Finsbury Park. This service commenced on 8 November 1976 and was augmented by the second stage from 3 October 1977, from Welwyn Garden City northwards through Hitchin to Royston. The full timetable came into effect on 6 February 1978, marking a temporary cessation of the long-standing through trains between King's Cross and Cambridge until the Royston-Cambridge section was energised a decade later, in the summer of 1988. Meantime electrification had been extended northwards along the main line, as far as Huntingdon from 3 November 1986 and then to Peterborough and beyond; an hourly semi-fast service between King's Cross and Peterborough commenced on 11 May 1987.

GN line up suburban services, 1961

To:	King's Cross	Finsbury Park	Moorgate	Broad Street	Total
Arrivals from: Gordon Hill	4	-	3	2	9
Cuffley	-	1	1	3	5
Hertford North	18	13	3	5	39
Wood Green	1	-	-	-	1
New Barnet	-	-	1	1	2
Potters Bar	2	-	2	-	4
Hatfield	13	1	1	1	16
Welwyn Garden City	16	3	2	1	22
Luton	1	-	-	-	1
Hitchin and beyond*	31	-	-	-	31
					130

* Including 24 from Baldock, Royston and Cambridge (stopping trains)

GN line down suburban services: comparative journey times

From London to:		Steam	Diesel	Electric
	Hertford North	57 mins	51 mins	45 mins (M)
	Hatfield	46 mins	40 mins	39 mins (M)
	Hitchin	72 mins	53 mins	42 mins (K)

M - from Moorgate; K - from King's Cross

The catenary was also in place at the northern end of the loop line, from Hertford North to Langley Junction, enabling the re-routing of the Huntingdon service via Hertford from the start of the 1990 summer timetable.

Initially the inner suburban off-peak service ran from and to Moorgate at 10-minute intervals, but from Winter 1987 it was reduced to four per hour, alternately serving Hertford North and Welwyn Garden City. Moorgate station's opening hours were curtailed with all early morning, late evening and weekend trains using King's Cross. The Winter 1993/94 timetable provided for 80 departures from Moorgate, of which 10 terminated at Finsbury Park and 10 went through to Stevenage via Hertford North. From King's Cross the off-peak service consisted of hourly trains to Peterborough, Letchworth, Royston and Cambridge, all running fast through the inner suburban area. Journey times by electric traction are of course less than in steam or diesel days, as shown for example in the accompanying table.

Traction and trains

From the early 1920s to the coming of the diesels, Gresley's Class 'N2' 0-6-2Ts were the backbone of the inner suburban motive power. Of the 107 locomotives built between 1920 and 1929, all but one were still at work in 1948. At that time the majority were stationed in the London area, with 57 at King's Cross shed, 10 at Hornsey, 14 at Hatfield and two at Hitchin. Most were condenser-fitted for working through the tunnels on the Widened Lines, virtually monopolising the traffic for which they were designed. The only exceptions were occasional turns worked by their Ivatt 'N1' predecessors, especially on Sundays, though even this was rare by 1950. Traditionally the

Above Waiting passengers look up from their newspapers to watch 'N2' 0-6-2T No 69584 struggling into King's Cross platform 16 from the depths of the Widened Lines with an evening train for Hertford North. The year is 1958, the last in which steam still had a monopoly of such activities. *F. Hornby*

Right Long before Wood Green became 'Alexandra Palace' this was a familiar sight many times daily as a condenser-fitted 'N2' 0-6-2T comes to a smart stop with its northbound train of 'Quad-art' stock. The date is 11 April 1953, and the locomotive still has ten more years of useful life ahead of it. *F. Hornby*

'N2s' worked chimney-first northbound, though this was uncomfortable for the crews on the sulphurous climb round the Hotel Curve into King's Cross. They worked long hours, frequently double-manned, some rosters including eight journeys spread over 14 hours. Their home at King's Cross was the seven-road 'Met shed' where some with regular crews were commendably well-kept. Withdrawal began in 1957 and their last regular duties were in 1960, though it was May 1962 before the last of the class left the London area.

In 1949 King's Cross shed received its first 'L1' 2-6-4T, of which nine were also allocated to Hitchin for outer-suburban duties. By the end of 1954 there were eight at 'Top Shed', and they ousted 'N2s' from some inner-suburban turns, although they were not permitted to

Soon after the introduction of five-coach rakes of BR standard suburban stock, 'N2' 0-6-2T No 69498 hurries past near Potters Bar on 17 March 1956 with northbound 'empties'. Misleadingly the locomotive still carries a 'New Barnet' destination board across the smokebox. *F. Hornby*

work to Moorgate or, until 1958, to Broad Street. Their career, inevitably, was much shorter than that of the 'N2s' although they still deputised for failed diesels up to 1961. By the end of 1960 the sole remaining turn rostered for steam was a peak-hour train from Broad Street to Potters Bar.

If Sir Nigel Gresley's name is honoured for his famous 'Pacifics' it may have been regarded with less reverence by the thousands who endured their daily travels in his 'Quad-art' sets, whose lifespan approximated to that of the 'N2s' that hauled them. First introduced on the GNR with accommodation in three classes and gas lighting, over 100 sets were built by 1929, the post-Grouping examples being electrically lit. The four coach bodies were articulated on five bogies with a substantial saving in weight, and a pair of 'Quad-arts' with 700 people on board weighed 182 tons tare, and thus around 235 tons gross. Overall length of a pair was 337 ft 5½ in, which, with locomotives, just fitted the terminal platforms at Moorgate. Although withdrawal in favour of BR standard compartment coaches began in 1955, they remained in service on peak-hour trains for a further 10 years, as five of the new BR coaches, seating only 468, was the maximum that Moorgate could accommodate. Hence the new vehicles, although more comfortable, provided far fewer seats, as did also their diesel unit replacements! From early BR days the 'Quad-arts' forsook their varnished teak livery for maroon, but the

lineage, to the end, was unmistakably 'Great Northern'.

On the steeply graded Alexandra Palace branch the peak-hour trains required the tractive power of an 'N2', but off-peak, with a two-coach set, ex-GNR 'C12' 4-4-2Ts sufficed, giving way in turn to ex-GCR engines of Classes 'F2' (2-4-2T), 'C13' (4-4-2T) and 'N5' (0-6-2T). Also used on the branch before closure in 1954 were 'N7' 0-6-2Ts transferred from Neasden. This class was also the normal motive power on the branches from Hatfield, where up to 15 were stationed; the Dunstable branch in particular was the preserve of these engines. The two-road shed at Hatfield (34C) closed in January 1961, followed by Hitchin (34D) in June.

Travellers by semi-fast trains experienced a wide variety of steam power over the years, even including, for a short time after nationalisation, the chance of a run behind one of the last surviving Ivatt 'C1' 'Atlantics' based at Hitchin. Eleven of their successors, the 'B1' 4-6-0s, were already established at that shed before 1948, working Cambridge line trains, and in 1950 one of them regularly double-headed with an 'A2/2' 4-6-2 on the 5.55 pm stopping train from King's Cross – 'super power' indeed!

Other classes participating in outer-suburban duties ranged from 'A4' streamlined 'Pacifics' and 'V2' 2-6-2s to the 'L1' 2-6-4Ts and a Fowler 2-6-4T loaned from the LM Region. Later, various engines were called on to substitute for diesels, until King's Cross 'Top Shed' (34A) closed in July 1963. *The Railway Observer* quoted, as examples in early 1963, a Class 'A3' on a Hatfield-King's Cross stopping train, a 'B1' on a morning train from Baldock, and a Class '4' 2-6-0 from Cuffley to Broad Street. Remarkably even in April 1964, a 'B1' from Peterborough was recorded on a morning train from Hatfield.

Diesel traction first appeared late in 1958 in the shape of both locomotives and multiple units. Servicing facilities for the locomotives were temporarily provided at the steam sheds until a six-road depot was ready at Finsbury Park in the spring of 1960, with a two-road sub depot at Hitchin.

Initially the locomotives were of three classes in the Type 2 power group, of which the first to arrive were 20 Birmingham RCW D53XXs, followed shortly by 10 North British Loco Co D61XXs and 10 English Electric 'Baby Deltic' D59XXs. The intention was to combine

Birmingham RCW 1,160 hp Bo-Bo diesel-electric No D5307 was only a few months old when entrusted with a Cambridge-King's Cross stopping train, seen here approaching Hatfield on 23 May 1959. Colour-light signalling is in evidence and the locomotive of a southbound freight can just be seen waiting in the loop. *F. Hornby*

	'TOPS' Class	Built	Year intro-duced	Wheel arrange-ment	Horse-power	Weight (tons cwt)	Max speed (mph)	Finsbury Park allocation 1965
Diesel-electric locomotive types employed on suburban duties								
Type 2								
D5000	24	Crewe/Derby	1958	Bo-Bo	1160	75 0	75	25
D5300	26	BRCW	1957	Bo-Bo	1160	77 10	75	-
D5500	31	Brush	1957	AIA-AIA	1365	104 0	75	49
D5900	23	English Electric	1959	Bo-Bo	1100	73 17	75	10
D6100	21	NBL Co	1958	Bo-Bo	1100	72 10	75	-
Type 1								
D8000	20	English Electric	1957	Bo-Bo	1000	72 0	75	10
D8200	15	BTH	1957	Bo-Bo	800	68 0	60	7

Viewed from the buffers at Moorgate on 3 April 1969, the near-empty platforms are deceptive as the 'evening peak' is in progress! On the left Brush Type 2 No D5641 has arrived with the stock to form the 17.31 to Potters Bar, while on the right Derby three-car diesel units make up the 17.41 to Hatfield. *J. M. Tolson*

suburban and empty stock duties with overnight freight trips to and from the Southern Region, but the Civil Engineer banned all three types from the latter function. In consequence the D53XX and D61XX Classes were exchanged for Derby/Sulzer D50XXs and the more powerful Brush D55XXs, while the D59XXs were outstationed at Hitchin. Sadly the latter gave a great deal of trouble and were withdrawn for overhaul in July 1963, returning to traffic the following year and used sporadically until retirement between 1968 and 1971.

Additionally two classes in the Type 1 category – English Electric D80XXs and BTH-built D82XXs – also saw service on the GN lines in small numbers. Neither were equipped for steam heating so were unpopular when deputising for other classes on suburban duties during the winter. They saw service on the Dunstable branch, with Hatfield's 'N7s' deputising during the winter until the shed closed, whereafter the Brush D55XXs took over during the branch's final years.

As in steam days, passengers using the outer-suburban services were treated to unusual haulage on occasions, even including the experimental locomotives DP2 and *Lion*, which, with 'Deltics' and 'Peaks', were recorded on Cambridge trains in 1964. At least once a 3,300 hp 'Deltic' gravitated to a Hertford North 'stopper' – presumably keeping time with ease! All the seven evening departures from Broad Street in the late 1960s were locomotive-hauled, the majority by the Class '31s'.

The first multiple units consisted of a fleet of 28 Class 105 Craven two-car diesel-mechanicals powered by 300 hp AEC engines and capable of 70 mph. They provided 12 1st and 103 2nd Class seats per unit and weighed 53 tons. Moorgate could only accommodate three units in multiple, with scarcely more than half the seats provided by a pair of the much-maligned 'Quad-arts'. Although the Cravens remained in a majority they were joined by Derby/BUT three-car units in the later 1960s and also by Derby/Rolls-Royce diesel-hydraulics. The 1970 allocation at Finsbury Park was made up of 46 Cravens, four Derby three-cars and 20 Derby/Rolls-Royce units. They were stabled and inspected at Finsbury Park Western Sidings, with the Rolls-Royce units visiting Stratford and the others Cambridge for periodical maintenance. By 1970 most had exchanged their original green livery for 'Rail Blue'.

At the commencement of the inner-suburban electrified services in November 1976 the Derby/Rolls-Royce units went into store and the Cravens' diagrams were reduced from 31 to 16 daily, but the three diagrams for the Derby three-car units were retained. There was a further reduction in the requirement for DMUs when the Hertford North-Stevenage section was electrified from 14 May 1979, and their last regular duties on GN lines were on the Hitchin and Huntingdon and Royston-

Above A Royston train comprised of Class 312 EMUs, with the first of the class, No 312001, leading, awaits departure from King's Cross main-line station on 27 May 1978. Similar in appearance to the pioneer Class 310s, they were built at York from 1975 and later renumbered in the 312700 series. *F. Hornby*

Right A Moorgate-Stevenage via Hertford North train sets down a few passengers at Palmers Green station on 4 October 1989. The 30-mile journey is allowed 58 minutes with 19 stops, making full use of the accelerative powers of graffiti-daubed EMU No 313050. *F. Hornby*

Cambridge sections until these also came under the catenary in 1986 and 1988 respectively. For these two services a small fleet of Metro-Cammell 'Low Density' two-car units (Class 101) was assigned.

For the inner-suburban electrification BREL at York built 64 three-car multiple units, Nos 313001-64, in 1976. Each unit weighed 103 tons, seated 230 and was powered by eight 110

hp GEC motors. As the 2.73 miles in tunnel from Moorgate to Drayton Park is electrified on the 750V DC third-rail system, while the surface mileage is on 25kV from overhead catenary, they are equipped with shoe gear on the outer bogies and a pantograph on the middle coaches. Changeover is made during the Drayton Park stop and the respective maximum speeds are 30 mph in the tunnel and 75 mph on

On 9 March 1993 a Class 313 EMU approaches Drayton Park, en route for Moorgate. During the stop the driver will lower the pantograph as 750V DC current will be collected from the third rail for the rest of the journey. The northbound track on the left burrows under the main lines in the background. *F. Hornby*

the surface. Power for the 25kV section is drawn from the National Grid at Wood Green and Welwyn Garden City.

The units are based at Hornsey where a six-road main shed and sidings are situated on the site of the old steam depot, with stabling sidings at Hertford North and Welwyn Garden City. When the services began 150 drivers were retrained from DMUs and there were 22 daily diagrams. Of the 64 units originally deployed, 44 remain on GN line duties, the remainder having been reallocated to the North London line.

The outer suburban service to Royston commenced in October 1977, worked by a batch of 26 new four-car Class 312 units modelled on the LM Region Class 310 prototypes. Built at BREL York in 1975-77,

they tip the scales at 151 tons, and their 1,080 hp motors give them a maximum speed of 90 mph. Seating capacity is for 297 in Standard and 25 in 1st Class accommodation. The full service came into effect in February 1978 and was operated by these units until 1986, when replacements from the LMR, in the shape of 100 mph Class 317s of 1981 design, first arrived at Hornsey depot. In March of that year Hornsey's roster included 23 Class 312 and seven Class 317 units, but in due course 72 units of sub-Classes 317/1 and 317/2 have completely ousted the 312s and have extended their activities to Peterborough and Cambridge. Interestingly, they also covered inner-suburban duties at weekends, when the Moorgate line was closed, for a 12-month period in 1989/90.

7.
NORTH LONDON LINES

Broad Street-Richmond and North Woolwich

The North London Railway, small in size but big in enterprise, was sponsored from its inception by the mighty London & North Western, and after entering into an even closer working arrangement in 1909, it was eventually absorbed by that company in 1922.

Although conceived with freight traffic in mind, as a link between the LNWR and the East London docks, it soon proved its value as a cross-London line for passenger traffic, and even by the 1860s was an archetypal suburban railway, running frequent trains at regular intervals long before that sensible principle was widely adopted elsewhere.

From early days its little 4-4-0Ts and four-wheeled carriages ranged far and wide well beyond the NLR, and at one time or another reached such diverse destinations as Windsor, Enfield and Plaistow. Some of these services were short-lived, but the trains continued to run on the Great Northern line throughout the Grouping era and, though discontinued during the Second World War, resumed in 1945 until the electrified service from Moorgate commenced in November 1976.

By nationalisation, however, much had changed and North London line services proper had been reduced to those initiated by the LNWR electric trains, first to Richmond in 1916, then to Watford in 1922. The service eastward to Poplar had ceased to run in May 1944 and it was largely thanks to GLC initiatives that stations were reopened and trains resumed running in 1979 – under the 'Crosstown Link' banner – with diesel multiple units between Camden Road and North Woolwich. Sufficient custom was attracted to warrant extension of the third rail to the new eastern terminus, reversing the relentless fall in patronage over many years, with the introduction of a North Woolwich to Richmond service – the 'North London Link' – from 13 May 1985.

It could be said, with the closure of Broad Street and the lack of success of the diversion into Liverpool Street, that the wheel had turned full circle, since the North London Railway's first services in the 1850s were along the east-west axis, just as are those of today.

Routes and infrastructure

The 'City Extension' to Broad Street, southwards for 2 miles from a triangular junction at Dalston, opened on 1 November 1865, climbing at 1 in 60 from Dalston Junction station on to a continuous viaduct alongside Kingsland Road and Shoreditch. Broad Street at its zenith was London's third busiest terminus, handling over 700 trains daily at its eight platforms by 1906, and over 40,000 passengers during the morning rush hours. Practically all the trains were strictly suburban, the only exceptions in BR years being some diversions from the GN main line during holiday weekends in 1951 and 1952 to relieve congestion at King's Cross.

By the 1920s five platform roads were equipped with conductor rails for the electric services, as were two of the four running lines to Dalston Junction; the two intermediate stations on this section were closed in 1940. During early BR years there was a steady decline in traffic, and in the late 1950s facilities at the terminus were reduced by closing the main block and substituting a small booking office on the concourse.

The decline continued to such an extent that by 1968, outside the peak hours, two men on duty sufficed to issue and collect tickets. Most of the train shed roof was removed and platforms 6 to 8 were closed in 1971. The remaining electrified line to Dalston Junction was lifted, one having already been dispensed with in 1966. The terminus proper fell into disuse in June

1985 and a single platform was substituted some 600 yards north, until final closure on 27 June 1986. The six-platform Dalston Junction closed simultaneously, an alternative station having opened some 2½ years previously on the east-west line at nearby Kingsland, at the same location as the original one of 1850!

Westwards from Dalston Junction four tracks were provided from 1871 as far as Camden Road Junction, all originally having platforms at the intermediate stations, although the northernmost pair were not electrified and so were for many years used exclusively for freight traffic. This was very heavy until the decline of the docks, whereafter one track has been lifted from Canonbury for over a mile through Caledonian Road & Barnsbury. From 18 April 1988 catenary at 25kV was energised from Camden Road over the freight lines and eastwards to Stratford, facilitating the replacement of diesel by electric locomotives on some freight trains. Thus the 4-mile section to the east of Canonbury is shared by 750V DC and 25kV AC traction.

Just east of Highbury & Islington the connection used by Great Northern line services until November 1976 diverges

northwards, passing through a quarter-mile tunnel en route to Finsbury Park. Between Caledonian Road & Barnsbury and Camden Road stations the North London crosses the main lines out of King's Cross and St Pancras on a high brick-arched viaduct. At Camden Road Junction one route, now used only by freight but formerly also by the Broad Street-Watford trains, continues straight ahead to join

North London lines from Broad Street to Dalston Junction, North Woolwich to Richmond, and Camden Road to Primrose Hill

Miles	Name	Opened	Closed	Notes
From Broad Street				
	Broad Street	11/1865	6/1985	
¼	(temporary station)	6/1985	6/1986	
2	Dalston Junction	11/1865	6/1986	
	Graham Road curve (to GE section) 6/1986-9/1992			
From North Woolwich				
	North Woolwich	6/1847		
¾	Silvertown & London City Airport	6/1847		'Silvertown' to 1987
1¾	Custom House	1855		
3	Canning Town	4/1846		Originally 'Barking Road'
3¾	West Ham	5/1979		
4½	Stratford Market	6/1847	5/1957	'Stratford Bridge' to 11/1880
4¾	Stratford (low level)	8/1854		
5¼	Hackney Wick	6/1850		Originally 'Hackney'; new station from 5/1980, original closed 4/1945
6½	Homerton	10/1868		New station from 5/1985; original closed 4/1945
7¼	Hackney Central	9/1850		New station from 5/1980
8	Dalston Kingsland	5/1983		Date for resited station; original open 11/1850 to 11/1865
9	Canonbury	12/1870		Resited station; 'Newington Road & Balls Pond' from 9/1858
9½	Highbury & Islington	9/1850		'Islington' to 1872
10	Caledonian Road & Barnsbury	6/1852		'Barnsbury' 1870-93
11	Camden Road	12/1850		'Camden Town' to 5/1950
11¾	Primrose Hill	6/1851	9/1992	Originally 'Hampstead Road' then 'Chalk Farm' to 9/1950
11¾	Kentish Town West	1/1860		Closed 4/1971-10/1982 following fire; 'West' from 1924
12¼	Gospel Oak	1/1860		'Kentish Town' to 2/1867
12¾	Hampstead Heath	1/1860		
13¾	Finchley Road & Frognal	1/1860		
14¼	West Hampstead	3/1888		'West End Lane' to 5/1975
14¾	Brondesbury	1/1860		
15	Brondesbury Park	6/1908		
15¾	Kensal Rise	11/1861		'Kensal Green' to 1890; second station opened 1873
16¾	Willesden Junction	9/1866		
18¼	Acton Central	8/1853		'Acton' to 1925

Miles	Name	Opened	Closed	Notes
19¼	South Acton	1/1880		
20	Gunnersbury	1/1869		'Brentford Road' to 11/1871
21	Kew Gardens	1/1869		
22¼	Richmond	1/1869		

Even the unsightly arcade of shops fails to conceal the architectural style of Broad Street station as completed in 1865. With nine platforms and 700 trains daily in its prime, the situation was very different at the time of this photograph in May 1974 when, outside business hours, few would-be passengers disturbed the peace. *F. Hornby*

On a wet day at Broad Street in May 1974 there is no protection for passengers beyond the first two coaches after the rest of the roof has been dismantled. A Class 501 EMU on a Richmond service is just visible on the left, while Craven DMUs on the right will form a peak-hour train for Hertford North. *F. Hornby*

the DC lines from Euston at Primrose Hill. The Richmond route curves north, crossing the Midland again beyond Kentish Town West, then swings west at Gospel Oak, the junction with the Tottenham & Hampstead line from Barking. The line then skirts Hampstead Heath, making a pleasant change from bricks and mortar, but immediately after the station of that name a three-quarter-mile tunnel penetrates the high ground of Hampstead.

Soon after emerging from the tunnel there is a third crossing over the Midland main line near West Hampstead, where the North London, Thameslink and Jubilee Line stations are conveniently close for interchange, and shortly afterwards the Chiltern Line and Metropolitan tracks pass overhead. The last major change of direction, to the south, is 2 miles further on at Willesden Junction high level, where the island platform is above and at

Left Dalston Kingsland station opened in May 1983 in anticipation of the closure of the nearby Junction station on the 'City Extension' to Broad Street. On 5 May 1993 it is host to dual-voltage unit No 313003 en route from North Woolwich to Richmond. *F. Hornby*

Middle left Highbury & Islington station provides an unsightly contrast of old and new architectural styles, with some remains of the original buildings on the right and the catenary for the freight lines visible beyond the fence on the left. This view is looking east on 20 April 1993. *F. Hornby*

Below Kentish Town West has had a chequered history as the old station was destroyed by fire in April 1971 and it was 11 years before a replacement was opened. A Richmond-bound Class 313 EMU departs on the left as another arrives en route to North Woolwich on 20 April 1993. *F. Hornby*

LONDON COMMUTER LINES

EMU No 313006 sets out from leafy West Hampstead station on 7 July 1993. The North London line can hardly be described as 'scenic', but the Hampstead area provides a small oasis in the otherwise unbroken vista of housing and industry east of Willesden Junction. *F. Hornby*

right-angles to the station for the Euston-Watford and Bakerloo Line trains; an electrified spur connects the high- and low-level lines, once used by an occasional Broad Street-Watford train. Then follows a veritable tangle of junctions where the North London crosses the main lines from Euston and Paddington together with the Central Line to West Ruislip.

The North & South Western Junction line from Cricklewood is joined at Acton Wells Junction and followed through the two Actons – Central and South – until it branches away to Kew Bridge. Then the District Line, on tracks of LSWR origin, is joined at Gunnersbury and North London and District Line trains share the remainder of the route to Richmond. They cross over the South Western Lines Hounslow loop and the River Thames at Kew before turning westwards for the final quarter-mile into Richmond. The station here has two terminal platforms for each of the two services, alongside the Windsor line through platforms. At this end of the line the stations are somewhat further apart and the aspect from the train is rather more pleasant than that eastwards from Willesden.

Retracing our steps to Dalston Kingsland, there are now eight intermediate stations in the 8 miles to North Woolwich, four of which were reopened in the 1980s for the 'Crosstown Link'. Half a mile east of Kingsland the Graham Road curve for the short-lived service between Watford and Liverpool Street diverges to the right, to join the line into the latter near

London Fields. Two miles further on the convolutions at Stratford are negotiated into the low-level station, at right-angles to the busy main station above. A mile to the south, the London, Tilbury & Southend route and District Line cross overhead at West Ham, with a footbridge linking the two stations. In traversing the still highly industrialised purlieus of Canning Town the tracks of the Docklands Light Railway Beckton branch (opened in April 1994) run parallel for a while. London City Airport is conveniently close to Silvertown station, though, by stark contrast to Gatwick, one doubts if much revenue is generated thereby!

The North Woolwich terminus, now reduced to a single platform, is close to the River; its fine old station building is now home to a museum dedicated to the Great Eastern Railway, as witness a 'plinthed' saddle tank outside.

The original North London Railway stations were quite impressive with tall if rather gaunt buildings in the mid-Victorian style. Little remains of these, though some stations do retain their protective awnings while others are reduced to steel-framed glass shelters. At the western end of the line several stations retain buildings at least partially intact – in particular Kew Gardens, which still displays evidence of its LSWR origins – while the genuine North London station house at Acton Central has survived as a pub!

In this age of high-tech signalling one must pay homage to the way the once numerous

Above The tracks at South Acton on 3 August 1993 could have benefited from a visit by the weed-killing train. Note the contrast in platform shelters at this unmanned station. The route-indicating signal on the right controls the junction of the lines to Richmond and to Kew Bridge, the latter for freight only. *F. Hornby*

Left It is a rainy scene at North Woolwich on 24 January 1985 as a Class 105 Craven DMU prepares to leave for Camden Road. The station building houses a museum dedicated to the GER, and a saddle tank locomotive undergoing restoration can be glimpsed on the left. *F. Hornby*

Left The erstwhile station building at Acton Central has at least escaped demolition in its new guise as a hostelry. Passengers have to be content with the narrow entrance on the left, but the eastbound platform still retains its sheltering roof. *F. Hornby*

This view of Brondesbury station looking east in February 1961 shows the fourth-rail system and, at the far end of the station, one of the then few colour-light signals. The viaduct in the distance carries the 'GC & Met' lines, while the signal box in the foreground, complete with fire buckets, is of vintage LNWR design. *B. W. Brooksbank*

manual boxes coped with the intensive flow of passenger and freight traffic, the latter still entirely steam-hauled until the late 1950s. By the 1960s there were pockets of colour-lights – notably along the 2-mile section east of Kensal Rise – with isolated automatic signals elsewhere. Special bell-codes were used to differentiate between the various routes, but by 1971 colour-lights had been installed in the Camden Road area and on the 'City Extension' to Broad Street. In recent years they have become universal and most boxes have closed, although some distinctive 'North London' boxes have survived, as at Dalston Kingsland and Camden Road.

As a footnote, at the time of writing plans are under consideration for the extension of 25kV electrification from Camden Road to Acton Wells Junction, together with the spur to Acton Main Line. The existing service is to be increased to four trains per hour and two new stations are to be provided between Willesden and Gunnersbury, together with platforms on the main slow lines at Willesden Junction. It would seem therefore that, at last, the North London line has effectively cast off its

reputation of being one of the 'Cinderellas' of London's rail network!

Services

Notwithstanding early electrification, the North London has always been a difficult line to work, particularly on the double-track sections shared with a sometimes unpredictable volume of freight traffic, while between Gunnersbury and Richmond there are the District Line trains to contend with. These days the problems have diminished with the freight traffic, which, thanks to diesel and electric traction, can dovetail in more easily with the EMUs.

Due attention was given to the Broad Street to Watford service when dealing with the DC line out of Euston, since both shared common trackage beyond Primrose Hill. Suffice it to recapitulate that in 1948 there were 33 weekday trains plus one to Rickmansworth, with a 5-hour gap from mid-morning onwards. The number increased to 44 on Saturdays with at least a half-hourly frequency until late evening, while on Sundays there were 17 trains

	North London line: 1948 journey times and speeds			
From Broad Street to:	Distance (miles)	Stops	Time (mins)	Average (mph)
Watford	22	23	60	22
Richmond	16¼	18	50	19½

each way during the afternoon and evening. Some trains omitted one or two stops, while a few – greatly daring – managed sprints, such as the weekday 4.50 pm, non-stop from Dalston Junction to Stonebridge Park!

The Richmond line notched up 50 trains each way on weekdays with an off-peak half-hourly frequency, and 55 on Saturdays, while on Sundays the attractions of Hampstead Heath and Kew Gardens were acknowledged by the provision of a 20-minute-interval service throughout most of the day. Hampstead Heath station in particular coped with large crowds on Bank Holidays in the pre-motor age. Save that Brondesbury Park was closed on weekday evenings and Sundays, the majority of trains were 'all stations'.

Additionally to the two electrified services, Broad Street received two steam trains from Tring and seven from Great Northern line stations on weekday mornings, and dispatched the same number in the afternoons. By the following year, 1949, Sunday services to Watford had been withdrawn, while on Saturdays some trains ventured no further than Willesden Junction.

Moving on to 1957, the overall picture had not greatly changed. Between 10 am and 2.30 pm there was a half-hourly service to and from Willesden, connecting with the Euston line for Watford, while on the Richmond line the 20-minute service on Sundays was still in place. Annual bookings at all North London line stations at this time were 4½ million and falling

– one tenth of the 1896 figure – so it is hardly surprising that it was earmarked for closure under the Beeching plan a few years later.

In 1963 the 20-minute interval was applied to the weekday services and the overall journey time was reduced by 4 to 8 minutes, though late evening trains were withdrawn. By 1966 the Sunday service was down to half-hourly and operated between 10.32 and 21.32 only, though with the introduction of the summer timetable the 20-minute frequency was restored throughout the day.

Management attitudes towards the line changed from time to time; for example, in 1952 fares were adjusted – upwards – so as to reflect more closely the distance travelled, resulting in a severe drop in patronage, but in 1972, faced with an annual loss of £367,000, a 'Crosstown' ticket was introduced, priced at 25p between any two stations. Later on, GLC involvement produced a subvention of £150,000 annually to maintain services at the 1975 level.

It was also thanks to GLC initiatives that the dieselised North Woolwich-Camden Road 'Crosstown Link' commenced on 14 May 1979 by diverting the former North Woolwich-Tottenham (Hale) service westwards from Stratford. There were 29 through trains each way daily, on weekdays only, at approximately half-hourly intervals off-peak. Journey time varied from 37 to 42 minutes for 11 miles with 10 intermediate stops. Would-be travellers were lured by introductory free tickets available

A Class 105 Craven two-car DMU has just arrived at Camden Road on its 'Crosstown Link' run from North Woolwich on 19 August 1981. The freight lines under the 25kV catenary and the remains of the old platforms can be seen on the far left. *F. Hornby*

from 14-18 May, and subsequent results were encouraging enough for a Saturday service to be added from July 1983.

Statistics for 1968 had showed that 9,000 passengers arrived at Broad Street on weekdays and a third as many on Saturdays, and it gradually became obvious that the days of the once-thriving terminus were numbered. In 1984 a start was made in laying conductor rails on the North Woolwich-Dalston Kingsland section in preparation for a through service to Richmond, which was inaugurated on 13 May 1985 under the title 'North London Link'. The honours were done by the former West Ham footballer Trevor Brooking. Meantime completion of the Graham Road curve enabled the remaining Broad Street-Watford trains (five up and six down) to be diverted to Liverpool Street from 30 June 1986. Possibly because of frequent cancellations, this service was never popular and survived only until 25 September 1992, by then reduced to just two trains each way.

So ended the 70-year history of the Broad Street-Watford service, leaving only the Richmond-North Woolwich link, running at 20-minute intervals throughout the day plus a few short workings (for example Willesden-Richmond and North Woolwich-Stratford) in the early and late hours. With 26 stops in 22¼ miles, the overall time is 67 minutes (23½ mph) – a modest improvement, at least, on the 1948 performance!

Traction and trains

For much of the period under review the traction situation on the North London line is identical with that on the DC line from Euston. In 1948 the ex-LNWR Oerlikon and LMS-built compartment stock EMUs operated both the Richmond and Watford services, and continued to do so until replaced by the Eastleigh-built Class 501s in the late 1950s. Until this time two units worked in multiple during peak hours, but enforced economies resulted in all services being worked by single three-car units throughout the day. Thanks to reductions in journey and turn-round times, and more regular intervals, it was found possible to

Two Oerlikon three-car units of LNWR origin await departure time for Richmond beneath Broad Street's lofty roof on 20 August 1955. The fourth-rail system of current collection will be noted – as will also the obligatory oil-lit tail lamp! *F. Hornby*

On 26 July 1980 a Class 501 EMU with barred toplights 'awaits the road' at Kew Gardens station before proceeding to Broad Street via Willesden Junction. On the BR and LT joint line, Kew Gardens was originally opened by the LSWR in 1869. *F. Hornby*

reduce the DC fleet from 105 LNWR/LMS units to 57 of the Eastleigh design. On the Richmond line eight trains, each made up of two three-car units, were needed up to 1962, and only five three-car trains thereafter.

The North Woolwich-Camden Road 'Crosstown Link' service of 1979-85 was operated by two-car Craven DMUs of Class 105 provided by Stratford depot, six units being rostered per day.

For the North Woolwich-Richmond 'North London Link' electrified service 15 two-car 2EPB (Class 416) units were transferred from the Southern Region, after bars had been fitted over the droplights because of restricted clearances in tunnels. They went into traffic on 13 May 1985, but it was claimed that their acceleration did not match that of the Class 501s, although their maximum speed of 75 mph was higher (and well in excess of that required on their new duties!). In consequence late running was not uncommon, when Richmond-bound trains were turned back at Gunnersbury. Their seating capacity was, of course, less than

the 501s at 186 as against 242 per unit. Perhaps no tears were shed when the time came for them to be replaced by the 1976-built Class 313 EMUs as also used on the Watford services. Although equipped for dual-voltage operation, their activities on the North London lines are wholly concerned with DC current collection from the third rail. There is no depot on the North Woolwich-Richmond line and they are based at Bletchley for maintenance purposes.

Until 1976 Broad Street station had witnessed a variety of motive power on the locomotive-hauled services to and from the Great Northern line and Tring, as has been touched on in the preceding chapters. 'B1' 4-6-0s and, later, 'L1' 2-6-4Ts were no strangers on the Eastern Region trains, to be supplanted by Type 2 diesels and eventually by Class 105 DMUs. At various times the main-line diesels Nos 10000/01 and 10201-03 appeared on the Tring duties, and on one occasion in August 1956 the pilot engine supplied by Willesden shed was a BR '9F' 2-10-0 – an impressive contrast to the usual diet of electric multiple units!

8.
LINES FROM LIVERPOOL STREET

The evolution of Liverpool Street's suburban services from the 1920s onwards could well be summed up by the tabloid-style heading 'From Jazz to Juice!' – the 'Jazz' being the popular name given to the intensive service introduced in 1920, and having nothing to do with the syncopated noises from a multitude of Westinghouse pumps! The 'Juice' came much later as electrification was delayed by the Second World War and did not embrace the whole suburban network until 1969.

But the story began much earlier as, by the time Liverpool Street opened in 1876, the Great Eastern Railway – successor to the Eastern Counties and Northern & Eastern companies – was already handling a thriving traffic generated by the rapid expansion of London's north-eastern suburbs. In 1894 the East Side Extension comprising platforms 11-18 was opened at Liverpool Street, by which time nearly 900 trains were being dealt with daily.

In the aftermath of the Great War this increased still further to 1,350, but while other railways turned to electrification in similar circumstances, the Great Eastern balked at the huge cost of such a project. By resignalling and track realignments it became possible to run a substantially improved service, in rakes of 16 four-wheeled carriages providing 848 seats per train. Almost miraculously this traffic was worked by small tank engines of 2-4-2 and 0-6-0 types, with a few new 0-6-2Ts just coming on stream. In the mid-1920s daily passenger usage fell from 244,000 to 200,000, then remained more or less constant during the LNER era. There was some alleviation immediately after the Second World War when, as with the GN lines, some routes were transferred to London Transport, in this case by eastward extensions of the Central Line. By December 1947 Woodford had been reached, with further developments, as we shall see, in early BR years. Electrification of the remaining BR suburban lines commenced in 1949 and was completed two decades later.

The rebuilding of Liverpool Street started in 1985 with the commensurate resignalling in mid-1988, and the virtually new station was 'opened' by HM The Queen on 5 December 1991. Despite a decline in traffic, partially due to the opening of the Victoria Line to Walthamstow in September 1968, the station still deals with over 1,000 trains daily, with some 60,000 people arriving and departing in the peak hours.

From April 1988 all lines out of Liverpool Street, together with those from Fenchurch Street, came under the jurisdiction of the new Anglia Region, the suburban services of course all being well within the boundaries of Network SouthEast.

WEST ANGLIA LINES

**Liverpool Street-Broxbourne
via Tottenham Hale
Broxbourne-Hertford East and
Buntingford
Hackney Downs-Cheshunt
via Seven Sisters
Edmonton Green-Enfield
Clapton-Chingford**

Routes and infrastructure

As a legacy from early days the suburban services out of Liverpool Street fall into two distinct groups, using separate sets of platforms on opposite sides of the station.

LINES FROM LIVERPOOL STREET

Ongar
Blake Hall
North Weald
BR until 1/1/1957
Epping
Theydon Bois
BR until 9/1949
Debden
Loughton
BR until 11/1948
Buckhurst Hill
Central Line (formerly GER)
Central Line LNER(NBR)
Chigwell
Grange Hill
To Chelmsford
Shenfield
Brentwood
To Southend

To Buntingford
To Bishops Stortford
Ware
Hertford East
St Margarets
Rye House
Broxbourne
Cheshunt
Waltham Cross
Enfield Lock
Brimsdown
Ponders End
Chingford
Theobalds Grove
Turkey Street
Southbury
Bury Street Junction
Bush Hill Park
Enfield Town
Edmonton Green
Silver Street
To Stevenage
North
Chase
Hertford Loop
GNR

To Upminster

LT&SR

Romford

Chadwell Heath

Goodmayes

Seven Kings

Newbury Park

1 Temple Mills East Junction
2 Clapton Junction
3 Copper Mill Junction
4 Spur removed 1964
5 Tottenham South Junction

Ilford

Flyover

Walthamstow Central

Manor Park

Forest Gate LT&SR

Maryland

To Barking, etc

Stratford

District Line

To Beckton

DLR

North Woolwich

To Poplar

LT&SR

Gas Factory Junction

Limehouse

T&FGJR

Lea Bridge

Temple Mills yard

Loco shed

NLR

Bow Junction

Seven Sisters

T&HJR

Gospel Oak

Stamford Hill

To King's Cross

Stoke Newington

Rectory Road

Clapton

Hackney Downs

London Fields

Cambridge Heath

Bethnal Green

LIVERPOOL STREET

Fenchurch Street

To Camden Road, etc

St James Street

South Tottenham

To

At London Fields station, 2½ miles from the terminus, preparations for electrification are well in hand in this early 1960 scene looking south. One of several stations with names deceptively suggestive of a rural setting, London Fields is now served by trains at peak hours only. *Lens of Sutton*

West Anglia and Great Eastern suburban lines from Liverpool Street

Miles	Name	Opened	Closed	Notes
From Liverpool Street (West Anglia lines)				
	Liverpool Street	2/1874		
1¼	Bethnal Green	5/1872		
1¾	Cambridge Heath	5/1872		
2½	London Fields	5/1872		Closed 11/1981-9/1986 (fire damage)
3	Hackney Downs	5/1872		
3¾	Rectory Road	5/1872		
4¼	Stoke Newington	5/1872		
5	Stamford Hill	7/1872		
5½	Seven Sisters	7/1872		
6¼	Bruce Grove	7/1872		
7¼	White Hart Lane	7/1872		
8	Silver Street	7/1872		
8½	Edmonton Green	7/1872		Originally 'Lower Edmonton'

Lower Edmonton-Angel Road opened 8/1872; closed to passengers 1939

Miles	Name	Opened	Closed	Notes
Enfield Town branch				
9¾	Bush Hill Park	1880		
10¾	Enfield Town	3/1849		
Southbury (Churchbury) loop				
10½	Southbury	10/1891	10/1909; re-opened 11/1960	'Churchbury' to 11/1960
12¼	Turkey Street	10/1891		'Forty Hill' to 11/1960
13½	Theobalds Grove	10/1891		
Lea Valley line				
3	Hackney Downs			
4	Clapton	7/1872		
6	Tottenham (Hale)	9/1840		'Tottenham' to 5/1968
7	Northumberland Park	9/1840		Originally 'Marsh Lane'
7¾	Angel Road	9/1840		Originally 'Water Lane'
10	Ponders End	9/1840		
10¾	Brimsdown	1884		
11¾	Enfield Lock	1855		
12¾	Waltham Cross	9/1840		Originally '& Abbey'; second station opened 1885
14½	Cheshunt	1846		New station opened 1891
17¼	Broxbourne & Hoddesdon	9/1840		New station opened 11/1960
Hertford East branch				
17¼	Broxbourne			
19	Rye House	5/1846		
20¼	St Margarets	10/1843		Station enlarged 1864
22¼	Ware	10/1843		
24¼	Hertford East	10/1843		

Miles	Name	Opened	Closed	Notes
Chingford branch				
4	Clapton			
5¾	St James Street	4/1870		
6¼	Walthamstow Central	4/1870		'Hoe Street' to 5/1968
7	Wood Street	4/1870		
8½	Highams Park	1873		'Hale End' to 10/1894
10½	Chingford	11/1873		New station from 9/1878
From Liverpool Street (Great Eastern lines)				
	Liverpool Street (east side)	4/1894		
4	Stratford	6/1839		
4½	Maryland	1873		Originally 'Maryland Point'
5¼	Forest Gate	1840		
6¼	Manor Park	1873		
7¼	Ilford	6/1839		
8½	Seven Kings	1899		
9¼	Goodmayes	1901		
10	Chadwell Heath	1864		
12½	Romford	6/1839		
13½	Gidea Park	12/1910		'& Squirrels Heath' to 2/1969
15	Harold Wood	1868		
18¼	Brentwood	7/1840		
20¼	Shenfield	1850		
From North Woolwich				
	North Woolwich	6/1847		
1	Silvertown	6/1863		
2	Custom House	1/1855		
3	Canning Town	4/1846		
3¾	West Ham	5/1979		
4¼	Stratford (Market)	10/1854		'Stratford Bridge' to 11/1880
5	Stratford (Low level)	8/1854		
8	Lea Bridge	1840	7/1985	
10	South Tottenham	1871		
10¾	Seven Sisters	7/1872		
Palace Gates branch				
10¾	Seven Sisters			
11½	West Green	1/1878	1/1963	
12½	Noel Park	1/1878	1/1963	'Green Lanes' to 5/1884, 'Green Lanes & Noel Park' to 1/1902
13½	Palace Gates	10/1878	1/1963	
Central Line from Ilford (Fairlop loop)				
1¾	Newbury Park	1903		
2½	Barkingside	1903		} To LT 31/5/48
3¼	Fairlop	1903		
3¾	Hainault	1903		
4¼	Grange Hill	1903		} To LT 21/11/48
5¼	Chigwell	1903		
6½	Roding Valley	1936		

Table continued overleaf

Miles	Name	Opened	Closed	Notes
Central Line from Stratford				
5	Woodford	1856		} To LT 21/11/48
6¼	Buckhurst Hill	1856		
7¼	Loughton	4/1865		
8½	Debden	4/1865		} To LT 25/9/49
10¾	Theydon Bois	4/1865		
12¾	Epping	4/1865		
Ongar line				
	Epping			
2½	North Weald	4/1865	9/1994	
4½	Blake Hall	4/1865	9/1994	} To LT 18/11/57
6¼	Ongar	4/1865	9/1994	

The West Anglia lines serving the north-eastern suburbs use platforms 1-6 on the west side of the station dating from 1876, and four tracks are available out through Bethnal Green, where they bear away from the Great Eastern lines, and on to Hackney Downs. The three stations on this stretch have platforms on the slow lines only and services to two of them – London Fields and Cambridge Heath – are confined to peak hours. At Hackney Downs the Enfield and Cambridge lines part company, with the latter veering to the north-east through two tunnels before joining the original route via Stratford at Copper Mill Junction. It then runs due north along the Lea Valley, throwing off a spur on to the Tottenham & Hampstead line at Tottenham South Junction en route. (Until 1964 this was used by the North Woolwich-Palace Gates service, which is discussed in the following 'Great Eastern' section.)

Tottenham Hale, the next station, offers interchange with the northern end of the Victoria Line, and has recently been modernised, being a stopping place for the 'Stansted Express' and Cambridge trains as well as for local services. Cheshunt (population 40,000) has a bay platform for Churchbury loop trains – of which more anon – and Broxbourne has a modern station that was opened in 1960 on a site 100 yards north of its predecessor. It consists of two island platforms, facilitating the splitting and joining of the

Hertford and Bishops Stortford sections of trains on the outer loops.

Chronologically the Lea Valley line was first in the field, opened in 1840 with branches from Angel Road to Enfield Town dating from 1849, and Broxbourne to Hertford East from 1843. The latter, 7 miles long, has four intermediate stations, the second of which – St Margarets – was until 1964 the junction for the Buntingford branch. This had opened in July 1863 with six small stations along its 13¾ miles, so just survived its century. It was very much on the periphery of the suburban area and Buntingford, with single platform, run-round loop and sidings, epitomised the 'country branch' terminus. Hertford East, by contrast, is still graced by an impressive 'period' station building and, in its heyday, had a spacious yard in addition to its two terminal platforms.

It was not until 1872 that the more direct route to Enfield was opened, northwards from Hackney Downs along gently rising gradients to Lower Edmonton (now Edmonton Green) where it joined the old line from Angel Road. This latter line lost its passenger service in 1939, since when all Enfield trains have been routed via Seven Sisters. Enfield, with a quarter of a million inhabitants, is, of course, also served by Enfield Chase station on the GN Hertford loop, but the ex-GER station is more central and in steam days had four platforms and a locomotive depot – one of Stratford's

Right Rebuilding is in full swing at Tottenham Hale station on 17 September 1991 as 'Stansted Express' EMU No 322483 pauses en route to Liverpool Street. The ultra-modern architectural style emphasises its importance as an interchange station with the Victoria Line and with local bus services. *F. Hornby*

Middle right Hertford East terminus is graced by a stylish building just visible in the background of this 26 October 1985 scene. Two generations of EMUs occupy the platforms, a '315' on the left and a '305' from two decades earlier on the right. *F. Hornby*

Below Edmonton Green, better known for most of its days as Lower Edmonton, is the junction station for the Enfield Town branch. On 25 January 1993 EMU No 315840 of 1980 vintage contrasts with the traditional GER style of the station canopies, which have survived on both platforms. *F. Hornby*

Enfield Town in steam days maintained a dozen or so 'N7' 0-6-2Ts at the small shed, a 'sub' to the huge depot at Stratford. On 20 September 1958 No 69662 is replenishing its water supply through a rather slender hose, in between journeys to and from Liverpool Street. *F. Hornby*

'sub-sheds'. The old station buildings were another of the casualties of the modernisation programme.

The Churchbury loop was opened in 1891 from Bury Street Junction on the Enfield line to Cheshunt, giving three new stations a direct service to London, but it was relatively short-lived, succumbing to tramway competition in 1909. Save for a period during the First World War when trains were run along it for munitions workers, it remained closed until 1960 when electrification gave it a new lease of life, with two of the three stations renamed.

On a parallel with Enfield as one of the West Anglia Lines' most important sources of revenue is the 6-mile Chingford branch, climbing steadily from Clapton Junction at 1 in 78 through four intermediate stations. Opened

Chingford is the terminus for arguably the busiest of all 'West Anglia' services, and there are extensive stabling sidings for EMUs when not in use. On 10 April 1989 the scene is dominated by Class 305 units in blue-grey livery. *F. Hornby*

throughout in 1873, its early claim to fame derived from the vast crowds of day-trippers bound for Epping Forest on high days and holidays. It currently more than earns its keep from commuters and off-peak patronage with interchange at Walthamstow Central for both the Victoria Line and an adjacent bus station. Motive power in steam days was provided by a sub-shed at Wood Street, Walthamstow, as well as by Stratford. Chingford terminus originally had four platform faces (of which three are still in use) and is a signing-on point for drivers of the EMUs that stable in the adjacent sidings.

Contracts were placed in 1957 for rolling-stock and equipment in anticipation of electrification to Enfield Town, Hertford East and Bishops Stortford via Seven Sisters, together with the Chingford branch. Work started in 1958 on erecting catenary, and in all 28 stations had their platforms lengthened to take nine cars in the inner and eight cars in the outer suburban areas. Bridges were raised or the trackbed lowered at many places to allow headroom for the catenary. The single-phase AC system was adopted, with a power supply of 6.25kV as far out as just south of Cheshunt – due to clearance problems – and 25kV beyond that point, so the multiple unit fleet was suitably equipped for both currents. Trains began running to steam timings on 14 November 1960 and a full service commenced a week later. In all 45 route and 111 track miles were converted.

The Lea Valley line between Clapton and Cheshunt (9 route miles) was added from 5 May 1969 using 25kV current beyond Copper Mill Junction, trial running having commenced in March, thus completing what is now the West Anglia suburban network. However, later on standardisation of the 25kV voltage was implemented; carried out in stages, it involved closure of the Clapton tunnels for three weeks, during which time the Hertford East and Bishops Stortford trains ran via Seven Sisters. The work was completed on 21 August 1983.

Even in pre-war days the intensive services on the Enfield Town and Chingford branches had warranted the installation of colour-light signals and continuous track-circuiting northwards from Bethnal Green in 1938-39. Post-war, in September 1949, a new box was opened at Liverpool Street, taking over complete control of the station with four-aspect colour-lights overseeing all six tracks. Beyond Bury Street Junction, Edmonton, semaphore signals were replaced by three- or four-aspect colour-lights in readiness for electrification, and the Broxbourne to Hertford East section was similarly equipped in January 1960. New signal boxes at Hackney Downs, in the angle of the junction, and at Ware and Broxbourne replaced most of the older boxes. When it was the turn of the Lea Valley line to follow suit the opportunity was taken also to re-signal the then unelectrified Tottenham-Stratford line, with Temple Mills West box taking over control of the Copper Mill Junction to Tottenham Hale section, while Cheshunt and Brimsdown boxes

The Network SouthEast livery adorns EMU No 315860, heading north from Brimsdown on the Lea Valley line on 19 January 1993. Generally straight and easily graded with the stations not too close together, modern units can show their paces more readily hereabouts than on the difficult sections closer to London. *F. Hornby*

were modernised. Much rationalising of tracks and sidings and improvements to stations was also carried out.

In recognition of its value as a diversionary route, the Stratford-Copper Mill Junction section was electrified in 1989, together with the South Tottenham-Seven Sisters spur. Resignalling in conjunction with the rebuilding of Liverpool Street commenced in mid-1988, but prolonged problems were experienced, and in the following spring there was such serious disruption that regular commuters were offered free rides by way of compensation! The 1949 box and the one at Bethnal Green were replaced by a new panel box, and by the end of May 1989 things began to settle down and all was functioning smoothly.

Services

In the early years of nationalisation both the Chingford and Enfield Town services were sufficiently intensive for *Bradshaw* not to consider it necessary to show detailed timetables. In 1949, for example, only the early morning and late evening trains were listed, those from Chingford commencing at 12.55 am and finishing at 11.50 pm with 'frequent intervals' covering the greater part of the day. There was no separate table for Saturdays, while Sunday trains ran at half-hourly intervals over a 16-hour period. Enfield Town fared slightly less well, as the first and last departures were at 4.11 am and 11.35 pm respectively,

with a half-hourly frequency outside peak hours and on Sundays.

Hertford East and Broxbourne services did warrant a detailed timetable as some trains used the direct route to Liverpool Street via Clapton (20 from Hertford East and two from Broxbourne on weekdays), while others were routed via Stratford, where some terminated. One train ran through from Hertford East to North Woolwich, while there were also two short workings from Hertford East to Broxbourne and one from Tottenham to Stratford.

Generally services remained at similar levels during the steam era, but in the 1954 summer timetable the Enfield Town off-peak frequency was stepped up to three per hour, one of which was semi-fast.

Electrification brought great improvements and a special timetable was issued commencing 21 November 1960 after a week of trial running to steam timings. In it the Chingford and Enfield Town services were combined; Chingford was endowed with no fewer than 126 weekday up trains, even the off-peak service being six per hour. Enfield Town also enjoyed the same frequency, inclusive of two trains per hour making all 13 stops and providing the only service for London Fields and Cambridge Heath. On Sundays both branches had quarter-hourly services between 9 am and 9 pm with earlier and later trains half-hourly.

In the table for Hertford East and Bishops

In the early days following electrification a pair of green-liveried Class 305/1 EMUs pause at Bush Hill Park on the Enfield Town branch in April 1961. Equipped for dual voltage, the train is collecting current from the catenary at 6.25kV on this section. *B. W. Brooksbank*

Summary of West Anglia suburban services

Year	Line	Route via	Distance (miles)	Stops	Time (mins)	Average (mph)	Traction
1949	Hertford East	Lea Valley	24¼	15	75	19.4	Steam
	Enfield Town	Seven Sisters	10¾	13	34	19.0	Steam
	Chingford	Clapton	10½	11	33	19.1	Steam
1960	Hertford East	Churchbury (Southbury) loop	24½	13	51	28.8	Electric
	Enfield Town	Seven Sisters	10¾	13	29	22.4	Electric
	Chingford	Clapton	10½	7	23	27.4	Electric
1966	Broxbourne	Lea Valley	17¼	9	36	28.75	Diesel
1993	Hertford East	Lea Valley	24¼	13	51	28.5	Electric
	Enfield Town	Seven Sisters	10¾	8	26	24.7	Electric
	Chingford	Clapton	10½	7	26	24.2	Electric
	Cheshunt	Churchbury (Southbury) loop	14½	13	38	23.0	Electric

Stortford we find that 5 minutes was allowed at Broxbourne for trains to divide or combine. From the first weekday up train at 4.18 am until the last at 11.18 pm there were 44 scheduled – more than twice as many as in steam days and appreciably faster, albeit with fewer stops. Note that these were now routed via the re-opened Southbury (former 'Churchbury') loop, leaving diesel stopping trains to serve the Lea Valley line. These comprised 40 southbound services, of which 14 – including two from Brimsdown – terminated at Stratford, with the remainder going to Liverpool Street via Clapton. The diesel timings were approximately 25 per cent faster than with steam traction.

While electrification work was in progress there had been some disruption, particularly at weekends, with, for example in March 1958, DMUs shuttling between Lower Edmonton and Enfield Town on Sundays in place of through trains. Then, needless to say, there were 'teething troubles' with the new equipment, causing cancellations when the units were withdrawn for modifications. Eventually a full service was restored on 17 June 1963 with strengthened trains providing extra seats, and that year in the afternoon peak there were no fewer than 67 departures scheduled hourly from Liverpool Street.

Over the ensuing years there has been some retrenchment from the lavish level of the early 1960s, a 'low spot' being at the end of 1981 when some timetable revisions coincided with a spate of train and signalling failures. More successful was the restoration of a 10-minute off-peak frequency to the Enfield line in 1983 (four per hour to Enfield Town plus two to Broxbourne or beyond). Harking back to the 1920s, the Class 305/1 EMUs were decorated with a colourful 'Jazz' label!

In the final BR timetable of 1993/94, weekday off-peak services on the Chingford and Enfield Town branches ran at 20- and 30-minute intervals respectively, while on the Lea Valley line electric stopping trains were allowed 1 minute longer than their diesel predecessors, but with more calls en route. The basic frequency to and from Hertford East was half-hourly, with the same number of Cambridge semi-fasts calling only at Tottenham Hale south of Cheshunt.

When inaugurated in 1969 the diesel service between North Woolwich and Tottenham Hale consisted of a dozen or so weekday trains in each direction, reduced to just four by 1981. In 1990, after the line between Copper Mill Junction and Stratford was electrified, an attempt was made to revive the service with a half-hourly 'shuttle' between Broxbourne and the new platforms 11 and 12 at Stratford; instead of reversing there, the trains were routed round the loop via the Channelsea and Fork junctions. Presumably due to lack of support, this venture lasted only two years before withdrawal.

Traction and trains

See page 124.

GREAT EASTERN LINES

Liverpool Street-Shenfield and North Woolwich-Palace Gates via Stratford
Stratford-Ongar and Newbury Park

Routes and infrastructure

By contrast with the West Anglia network, the only 'Great Eastern' service remaining operative is that along the main line through Shenfield. The Palace Gates branch from Seven Sisters closed in 1963, the remainder of the line to Ongar and the Fairlop loop have been absorbed by the Central Line, and a Stratford-Broxbourne service introduced in October 1990 was discontinued in less than two years.

At Liverpool Street all Great Eastern suburban trains use the east side platforms Nos 11-18, which, in the course of rebuilding, have been covered by a low roof supporting a raft of offices, whereas the remainder of the station enjoys the splendour of the restored train shed.

The Eastern Counties main line, originally of 5-foot gauge, opened to Romford in 1839 and on to Colchester in 1841, and was converted to standard gauge in 1844. It became part of the Great Eastern Railway in 1862.

Local trains use the southernmost pair of tracks up the 1 in 70 Bethnal Green bank and out through Stratford to Ilford, where the flyover constructed in readiness for the post-war electrification carries them to the opposite side of the main lines. There is a steady climb for 14 miles from just beyond Stratford, steepening for the final 3 miles on average to 1 in 100 – presenting in steam days quite a challenge to game little tank engines with a pair of crowded 'Quint-arts' in tow.

Since December 1946, when Coborn Road closed, Stratford has been the first station out of Liverpool Street on the line under discussion. It has become progressively more important as an interchange station, with the Central Line emerging briefly on to the surface giving cross-platform connection and – more recently – the Docklands Light Railway having a bay in the up island platform. Two new platforms, Nos 11 and 12, were provided for the Broxbourne shuttle service, and now, regrettably, stand disused. As given due notice in the previous chapter, there are two platforms below and at right-angles for the North London line.

Stratford's interchange facilities are emphasised by this scene on 5 March 1980 as a Central Line train of 1960 stock bound for Epping emerges from the tunnel. Alongside, en route for Liverpool Street, is a Class 305 EMU as built in 1960 for 6.25kV or 25kV AC current collection. *F. Hornby*

This view at Ilford looking north on 5 May 1993 gives some idea of the generous proportions of Shenfield line suburban stations. Class 315 unit No 838, bound for Gidea Park, is one of the 64 of this type based and maintained at the nearby depot. *F. Hornby*

On 15 October 1956 at Palace Gates, 'N7' 0-6-2T No 69613, with a 'Quint-art' set in tow, forms the 12.31 to North Woolwich. The branch closed to passenger traffic in 1963, and the substantial station with its tall chimney stacks is now but a memory. *F. Hornby*

Of the 11 stations in the 16¼ miles on to Shenfield, with platforms for all four running lines, the most important are Ilford and Romford (pop 75,000), the latter being served by Colchester semi-fast trains as well as by the 'locals'. Harold Wood and Forest Gate stations were modernised in 1985/86 as a joint GLC/BR venture. Shenfield, where some services terminate, is the junction for the line to Southend and Southminster, which parts company from the Colchester main line just beyond the station by means of a burrowing junction.

The Stratford-Palace Gates service was a magnet for enthusiasts, not only because of the motive power used at various times, but also because it passed close to the locomotive sheds, then through the extensive and busy Temple Mills yards. Sadly only a few weed-grown sidings remain where once a small army of shunting engines worked round the clock. The line crosses the Hackney and Walthamstow marshes and the Warwick reservoirs, then a sharply curved spur leads to the 'Tottenham & Hampstead', which was followed through South Tottenham station before taking another 90-degree curve into Seven Sisters.

Here the Palace Gates branch proper began, with its own two platforms where it swung away to the north-west. It was 2¾ miles long with two intermediate stations, and had an active life of 85 years, from 1878 to 1963, with freight traffic lingering until October 1964. A direct connection to the GN Hertford loop, installed in 1944 in place of a less convenient shunt spur, was useful for transferring stock (and was covered by the author on a memorable railtour, hauled by an ex-GER 'E4' 2-4-0!).

The line south of Stratford was a good deal older and was opened throughout to North Woolwich, close to the Royal group of docks, in June 1847 with connections for ferries and steamers. In 1880 the line was diverted into a tunnel under the waterway linking the Royal Victoria with the newly opened Royal Albert dock; a journey along it in steam days was fascinating as, not only was there a heavy freight traffic, but Port of London Authority tank locomotives could also be seen. The line remained an outpost of semaphore signalling when colour-lights were the norm elsewhere, and because of sharp curvature was renowned for the wear and tear inflicted on rolling-stock. The terminus, once generously laid out with two island platforms and a centre engine release road, now consists of but a single platform.

During 1948 and 1949 the Central Line was further extended along former BR tracks through Loughton to Epping. A new line in tunnel from Leytonstone to Newbury Park, connecting with the Fairlop loop, had opened in December 1947 and the remainder of the loop was converted the following year. The old GER line, northwards to Newbury Park from a triangle junction east of Ilford, was abandoned on 30 November 1947 and a bus service substituted until the work was completed. All this left the 6¼-mile Epping-Ongar section isolated from the rest of BR, and it remained steam worked until electrified in November 1957. Since then the tube stock has looked slightly incongruous, scuttling along the single-track line through open countryside with two intermediate stations. In steam days the terminus at Ongar had a small engine shed and goods yard alongside the single platform.

Barkingside on the Fairlop loop remained in BR hands until May 1948, but the London Transport 'bullseyes' confirm that this photograph is of later origin. Taken on 1 April 1961 it is a pleasing reminder that the Central Line has, in many cases, retained the old pre-Grouping railway station buildings in good order. *B. W. L. Brooksbank*

Epping station on 20 October 1956 provides a contrast between the old and the 'not quite so old'. Class 'F5' 2-4-2T No 67200 is a rebuild of a GER Worsdell creation of 1904, heading a two-coach 'auto' set from Ongar. The Central Line train, about to undertake a lengthy cross-London journey to West Ruislip, is of pre-war 1936 stock. *F. Hornby*

LONDON COMMUTER LINES

The LNER, having operated one of the world's most intensive steam-worked services since its formation, decided in 1936 to electrify the main line out as far as Shenfield, but the work was interrupted by the outbreak of war and was eventually completed by BR on 26 September 1949. All four running lines over the 20¼ miles were equipped with overhead catenary for 1,500V DC current, as were platforms 11-18 at Liverpool Street and also the two tracks from Bow Junction into Fenchurch Street. Preparatory work included layout rearrangements, extensive rebuilding of Stratford station, and the flyover between Manor Park and Ilford. Four-aspect colour-light signals were installed out to Gidea Park, beyond which point they were already in place to Chelmsford. Nine new and three modernised signal boxes replaced 33 old mechanical ones; the new signalling permitted 1½-minute headways and a maximum speed of 75 mph. A depot with repair facilities for the new trains was opened at Ilford, and subsequently enlarged in 1959 to cope with additional stock.

The 1,500V DC catenary was extended to Chelmsford in June 1956 and to Southend by the end of the year, but in November 1960 the power supply was changed to 6.25kV AC between Liverpool Street and Shenfield, and to 25kV AC eastwards to Chelmsford, with services maintained by a mixture of diesel and electric trains and buses during the changeover weekend. Electrification was further extended to Colchester in mid-1962, where it linked up with the existing 25kV lines to Clacton and Walton, which had been energised for trial purposes in April 1959. In the opposite direction the conversion to 25kV advanced towards London from Shenfield in stages, commencing in January 1976 and completed into Liverpool Street on 12 October 1980, with the Shenfield-Southend line similarly converted in January 1979.

Services

Steam timings out to Shenfield in the late 1940s fluctuated between 48 minutes and 1 hour depending on the number of stops. Trains ran at 'frequent intervals' throughout the day (stopping trains were every 20 minutes off-peak) and the principal stations – Stratford, Ilford and Romford – also benefited from calls made by semi-fasts for destinations as far down the line as Ipswich or Clacton.

Nevertheless the 1949 electrified service provided more and faster trains even if the new units could hardly compete with the old steam stock in the matter of seating the maximum number of bodies in the minimum of space! The first electric train to Shenfield ran on 26 September and the full service commenced on 7 November – only to be disrupted during the first morning rush hour when the catenary was brought down at Seven Kings! On the same day the peak-hour service between Fenchurch Street and Ilford was withdrawn, although the connecting line from Bow Junction was electrified and made use of during emergencies – as when floods blocked the LT&S Southend line in February 1953.

The first timetable featuring the full service listed 62 weekday electric trains to Shenfield, with three per hour off-peak, semi-fast as far as Romford and all stations thereafter. Gidea Park was the outer terminus for 65 more trains, running every 20 minutes and calling at all stations. The earliest and latest trains out of Liverpool Street were still steam-hauled, as was of course the Southend service, which provided Shenfield with a further 37 weekday down trains – a grand total of 101 in 24 hours! On Sundays four electrics left the terminus hourly – two each to Shenfield and Gidea Park. Journey time to Shenfield was down from 55-60 minutes in steam days to 38 minutes.

Fourteen steam trains each way covered the 12½ miles between Palace Gates and North Woolwich (11 on Saturdays), averaging 48 minutes en route with 10 stops, with two others between North Woolwich and Lea Bridge and one in the opposite direction; these trains were valuable for those living in the northern suburbs and working in the docks. A shuttle service along the branch from Seven Sisters supplemented the through trains and, unlike them, operated on Sundays. At the other end of the line 26 trains plied between North Woolwich and Stratford, including two that continued northwards along the Lea Valley line, balanced only by one southbound working. As the author discovered purely by chance, at least one train was extended northwards from Stratford, unadvertised, when 'Spurs' were at home on Saturday afternoons!

The Palace Gates branch closed in 1951 due to fuel shortages, and though it reopened later on, the shuttle service from Seven Sisters was not resumed.

Electrification to Southend and Chelmsford resulted in double the number of passengers within a year, and in consequence fewer trains terminated at or started from Shenfield. In the summer of 1961 that town was served by 120 weekday trains daily from Liverpool Street, of which only 20 terminated there – generous indeed as the population was then no more than 5,000! By then the Gidea Park stopping service was only half-hourly, with three other trains calling there hourly to and from Southend.

In 1962 there were still six through trains between Palace Gates and North Woolwich plus 30 southwards from Stratford, but the branch from Seven Sisters closed to passengers and the gradual move towards a five-day week saw the withdrawal of Saturday trains between Stratford and North Woolwich in January 1969.

In 1949 the Epping-Ongar section boasted a shuttle-service of 35 weekday and Saturday trains each way and 26 on Sundays. Journey time for the 6¼ miles was 16 minutes with two intermediate stops. The connecting Central Line trains gave a frequent service, taking 40 minutes to and from Liverpool Street. When electrification reached Ongar in November 1957 there were initially more trains, but in recent years only a sparse peak-hour service penetrated beyond Epping, and a 1980 census revealed that a mere 650 passengers were using the trains daily. In the present climate, in which London Underground Lines are constantly seeking to reduce costs, it is not surprising that this service was withdrawn from 30 September 1994.

Traction and trains (both lines)

The backbone of suburban operations out of Liverpool Street – all steam-worked at nationalisation – was the Class 'N7' 0-6-2T, of which the first 12 had appeared in 1921 in GER colours. Another 122 were in service by 1928, slightly smaller than their 'N2' counterparts of GNR origin and with smaller driving wheels. They were, however, sturdy machines and a distinct improvement over the Edwardian 'F5' and 'F6' 2-4-2Ts, of which a number were still at work in the London area into the 1950s.

The Shenfield electrification in 1949 brought some relief to the hard-pressed motive power department, confining the older engines to such relative backwaters as the North Woolwich and Epping-Ongar lines. Nevertheless an 'F5' made a 'comeback' on a Chingford train in August 1952, and as late as 1954 two 2-4-2Ts were noted on early Sunday morning through trains from Epping to Liverpool Street.

While all engines were nominally allocated to the huge shed at Stratford (30A), in practice the sub-sheds had fairly permanent studs of 'N7s' – 14 at Wood Street, Walthamstow, 10 at Hertford East and 12 at Enfield Town. By 1950 Stratford had also acquired a fleet of 33 recently built 'L1' 2-6-4Ts, which were employed on outer suburban duties such as to Bishops Stortford and Hertford East, also working further afield on extra trains at summer weekends. Their numbers at Stratford were later reduced and remained constant at around 20 for several years thereafter. Similarly the 'N7' allocation diminished thanks to electrification and the introduction of DMUs on the Lea Valley line.

Nine engines were maintained at the two-road shed at Palace Gates, inclusive of three 'G5' 0-4-4Ts from the North Eastern area, which worked the two-coach 'push-pulls' until transferred away in 1951. On a visit made by the author in November 1949 an 'F5' powered an articulated set out to Palace Gates and a 'G5' worked a two-coach train in the opposite direction. The return fare from Liverpool Street was 1 shilling (5p)!

With the departure of the 'G5s' and the withdrawal of the 'F5s', the 'N7' tanks were left in sole charge, as was also the case during the last years of steam working between Epping and Ongar. By 1961, when most 'N7s' had joined the sad procession to the scrapyard, the 'L1' 2-6-4Ts were 'regulars' on the North Woolwich trains.

One of the stalwarts of the London suburban services, Class 'N7' 0-6-2T No 69720 comes off the line from Clapton at Hackney Downs with a stopping train from Hertford East on 20 September 1958. The stock consists of compartment coaches somewhat 'up market' from the traditional articulated sets. *F. Hornby*

With Stratford's vast and varied allocation it is hardly surprising that other classes deputised for failed engines, and in February 1953 Class 'J15' 0-6-0s were noted on early morning Hertford East trains. On the same line a rare stranger in 1957 was an ex-LT&S '3P' 4-4-2T, while in September 1959 a 'J69' 0-6-0T abandoned its Liverpool Street pilot duties for a foray on to the Chingford branch. Early in 1960 a locomotive shortage saw ex-LMS '3F' 'Jinty' 0-6-0Ts filling in on Hertford East trains – to the detriment of punctuality, one must assume. August 1956 had seen the equally unusual appearance of an 'N2' 0-6-2T and a BR Class '4' 2-6-0 on the Epping-Ongar 'shuttle'. Both were fitted with trip-cocks as required for working over LT tracks, but not with the push-pull gear of the regular motive power.

As for coaching stock, the GE section of the LNER went one better than the GN with 'Quint-art' sets – five coach bodies articulated on six bogies – as introduced by Gresley in 1924 to replace older bogie coaches of GER design. There were, however, also 'Quad-arts' of 1929 vintage for the longer-distance Hertford East trains, while the Bishops Stortford semi-fasts were graced with LNER-built compartment and part-corridor stock. When first built the 'Quint-arts' catered for three classes of accommodation, seating 872 in a 10-coach formation, but ultimately became 'all 3rd'. So, with standees aboard, our game little 65-ton 'N7' tanks would be tackling Bethnal Green bank with some 280 tons in tow.

Steam traction was finally abolished in September 1962, prior to which 'L1s' and surviving 'N7s' still worked a few turns on the North Woolwich branch, by then with outer-suburban coaches in place of articulated sets.

Since the Shenfield electrification there has been a considerable variety in the ever-growing fleet of electric multiple units, of which the first were the 92 dark green 1,500V DC three-car sets that became Class AM6 and later 306. With open saloons, push-button sliding doors and ample provision for 'straphangers', they were more akin to London Transport stock

On 7 June 1959 smart 'N7' 0-6-2T No 69665 wheels a 'Quint-art' set past Stratford on an Enfield Town train, diverted because of engineering works. It will regain its route via the line through Lea Bridge, thence via the 'Tottenham & Hampstead' and the curve into Seven Sisters. *F. Hornby*

than to the steam trains they replaced, and a nine-car train could seat 528 with another 660 standing. They were converted for AC current in 1960, but rarely strayed from the Shenfield main line and gave over 30 years of yeoman service, their last day on normal duties being 15 September 1981.

When the 1,500V DC catenary was extended beyond Shenfield in 1956, 32 units of Class AM7 (later 307) were delivered from Eastleigh, not surprisingly having an affinity with contemporary Southern Region flat-fronted designs. They were similarly converted for AC power supply in 1960-62 and have since been refurbished. They later diversified their activities by visits to the Hertford East line, and continued in service on the GE section until June 1990.

For the west-side suburban electrification –

today's West Anglia lines – 72 units were delivered in 1960 from BR York and Doncaster with English Electric equipment, comprising 52 three-car units (Class AM5/1 – later 305/1) and 19 four-car (Class AM5/2 – later 305/2), the latter being intended for Hertford East and Bishops Stortford services, with some 1st Class seating. They differed considerably from the Shenfield units, with sloping ends and slam-doors to each seating bay. While the 75 mph maximum of both sub-classes might be of advantage on the longer runs, it would be more than adequate on the sharply curved and steeply graded Chingford branch!

As mentioned, problems were experienced when they first went into service, and other units were loaned from the LTS section during late 1960. Also seen, around 1962, were AM4 units loaned from the LMR with 'Crewe' on

Goodmayes is traditionally the terminus for inner-suburban stopping trains, but this one is continuing to Shenfield. Led by No 041, a trio of Class 306 units in 'Rail Blue' livery are seen on 14 April 1979. It would be interesting to know how many miles they had clocked up on this same stretch in the previous 30 years! *F. Hornby*

Eastern Region EMU dimensions

Class	Introduced/ builder	Traction motors	Voltage	Max speed (mph)	Weight (tons)/cars per unit	Seating (1st/2nd)
AM2 (302)	1959 BR Doncaster/York	4 x 192 hp EE	6.25kV, 25kV	75	155/4	19/344
AM5/1 (305/1)	1960 BR York	4 x 200 hp GEC	6.25kV, 25kV	75	119/3	-/272
AM5/2 (305/2)	1960 BR Doncaster	4 x 205 hp GEC	6.25kV, 25kV	75	153/4	19/344
AM6 (306)	1949 Metro-Cammell/BR	4 x 207 hp Crompton Parkinson	1,500V DC, 6.25kV, 25kV	70	104/3	-/168
AM7 (307)	1956 (reb't 1960) BR Eastleigh	4 x 175 hp GEC	1,500V DC, 6.25kV, 25kV	75	155/4	19/344
AM8 (308)	1961 BR York	4 x 192 hp English Electric	6.25kV, 25kV	75	154/4	19/344
315	1980 BREL York	8 x 110 hp Brush	25kV	75	102/3	-/318

In this September 1991 view of Liverpool Street prior to rebuilding, two distinct designs of EMU stand side by side in the West Side suburban platforms. On the left, flat-fronted four-car unit No 302 505 is of type AM2 introduced in 1959 for the Tilbury section. On the right, Class 305/1 No 437 was a product of BR York in 1960 for the Chingford and Enfield lines. *F. Hornby*

With four-digit headcode blind prominent, four-car unit No 302201 leads a Southend semi-fast past Bethnal Green on 13 September 1981. The platforms at this station have since lost their canopies, and serve only the West Anglia local lines. *F. Hornby*

In 1977 BREL at York outshopped a batch of 19 EMUs of Class 312, as previously employed on the GN section, for residential services on the Great Eastern lines. No 312790, seen here at Shenfield on 25 September 1980, is on a Colchester-Liverpool Street working, and will call only at Romford on a smartly timed sprint up to Town. *F. Hornby*

The 'modern image' with a vengeance at Ilford! Up and down trains of the 100 mph Class 321 EMUs make a brief stop, with an 'inner-suburban' Class 315 unit in the background. *F. Hornby*

their destination blinds! Again, in 1965/6, when the AM5/2 series had a high failure rate, they were transferred to the LTS section in exchange for nine AM8/1 units, built at York in 1961, similar in appearance and also with dual-voltage capability. Another LTS-based type, the flat-fronted AM2 four-car units of 1959 vintage, made their appearance on the Lea Valley line after it was electrified in May 1969.

By mid-1973 Ilford depot's allocation consisted of 236 EMUs embracing Classes 302, 305/1, 305/2, 306, 307 and 308. The gradual elimination of 1960s designs was given impetus by the arrival of 19 new outer-suburban Class 312 four-car sets in 1979, all based at Clacton and employed on Colchester and Southend line services, joined in due course by the similar Hornsey-based '317s', which are used indiscriminately on inner- and outer-suburban duties.

The year 1980 ushered in a new era when the first of 61 four-car units of Class 315 came off the production line at BREL York and took up their duties on the Shenfield line as replacements for the aging Class 306. These all-Standard Class units were designed solely for 25kV power collection, with push-button-operated doors and inter-coach gangways, and extended their activities to all lines when conversion to the higher voltage was completed. In 1981 there were 44 weekday diagrams for the 315s, supplemented by 18 for Class 306s until the latter were retired later in the year; Class 308 units were transferred back to the LTS section from whence they had come.

In the present decade the 1990-design Class 321 units have taken a major share of the longer runs, with 66 of series 321/3 and a few of series 321/4 stationed at Ilford, so that most of the fleet now dates from the late 1970s onwards.

The role of the diesel unit on GE suburban duties was comparatively low-key, and the main sphere of operations was on the Lea Valley line and – at first alongside steam traction, then in full possession – on the North Woolwich service. The first appearance of DMUs was in the spring of 1956 when the two-car sets made driver-training runs on the Palace Gates branch and elsewhere. Wickham railcars performed briefly on that branch on Whit Monday 1958, but the first serious application was on Hertford East services from January 1959, when Derby/Rolls-Royce three-car suburban sets came into use. From 1962 they were responsible for most North Woolwich duties and continued to work on this branch before and after diversion along the North London line in 1979. Ex-WR three-car suburban sets were based at Stratford from September 1968, but DMU duties declined with the Lea Valley electrification in 1969. In 1977 there were just three two-car units on the roster for the North Woolwich-Tottenham Hale shuttle.

A further use was found for DMUs while conversion from 6.25 to 25kV power was carried out during October 1980, when they covered Liverpool Street-Hackney Downs runs, supplemented by units from Cricklewood. When they were no longer required for passenger purposes a few units could still be seen in the suburban area converted for express parcels duties, in a dark blue livery with orange stripes.

9.
LINES FROM FENCHURCH STREET

Fenchurch Street-Shoeburyness via Upminster
Barking-Pitsea via Tilbury
Romford-Upminster-Grays

In compiling this work the author has become increasingly aware that the term 'London Suburban' covers a wide spectrum, with at one extreme, for example, the Chingford branch with its closely spaced stations, and at the other the Chiltern Line, terminating at Aylesbury, nearly four times as far away. The LT&S section has something in common with the latter, both having comparatively small termini and both being overwhelmingly concerned with 'outer suburban' traffic. However, the territory served by the LT&S could hardly be more different, ranging from the dormitory towns centred on Southend, to the docks and industry around Tilbury and Dagenham. Virtually all trains from Fenchurch Street set out on journeys of between 22 and 45 miles, many being non-stop to Barking, 7½ miles out. Even in steam days, once the District Line had annexed the intermediate stations out to Upminster, most trains could be correctly described as 'semi-fast'.

This was self-evident in the motive power provided from early years, with several classes of 4-4-2Ts, not forgetting Whitelegg's massive 4-6-4Ts of 1912 which were deemed too heavy to work into Fenchurch Street!

As to ownership, we recall that the London terminus was Great Eastern property until the 1923 Grouping and LNER thereafter, although most of the trains using it were those of the London, Tilbury & Southend Railway until that company was absorbed by the Midland Railway in 1913 and in turn by the LMS in 1923. At nationalisation the Tilbury section first became part of the London Midland Region, then was transferred to the Eastern

Region in February 1949, and in 1986 became an important constituent of Network SouthEast. Now, as a largely self-contained entity, it could well become one of the first BR lines to be privatised.

Notwithstanding electrification in the early 1960s, the 'Tilbury', with its ageing infrastructure, has unfortunately become a byword for breakdowns, cancellations and delays. One can only hope that at least some of its long-suffering regular users appreciate the valiant efforts of hard-pressed staff who keep the wheels turning in extremely difficult circumstances.

Routes and infrastructure

Fenchurch Street station opened in 1841 as the terminus of the London & Blackwall Railway and was linked to the Eastern Counties Railway in 1854. A new and enlarged station was completed in that year, incorporating the building that has survived to the present day. The first LT&SR trains entered it over a newly laid direct line from Barking in March 1858. Ownership passed into the hands of the GER, as successors to the Eastern Counties Railway, in 1869, with the LT&SR exercising running powers into it from Gas Factory Junction. The direct route to Southend via Upminster was completed in June 1888, prior to which the longer route via Tilbury, dating from 1856, had been used.

A connection with the Metropolitan District Railway at Campbell Road Junction, Bromley-by-Bow, was opened in 1902 and District electric trains took over much of the shorter-

Suburban lines from Fenchurch Street (LT&S section) to Shoeburyness via Upminster, Pitsea via Tilbury, and branches from Upminster

Miles	Name	Opened	Closed	Notes
From Fenchurch Street				
	Fenchurch Street	8/1841		
1¾	Limehouse	7/1840		'Stepney East' to 5/1987
3¼	Bromley-by-Bow	1858		'Bromley' to 5/1967
4½	Plaistow	1858	To LTE	
5¼	Upton Park	1895	control 1970	
6¼	East Ham	1858		
7½	Barking	3/1858		
Tilbury loop				
10½	Dagenham Dock	7/1908		
12½	Rainham	1854		
15¼	Purfleet Rifle Range halt	1911	5/1948	
16	Purfleet	1854		
19¾	Grays	1854		
21½	Tilbury Town	1885		'Dock' to 12/1934
22½	Tilbury Riverside	1854	12/1992	'Tilbury' to 7/1936
24¼	Low Street	1861	6/1967	
25¼	East Tilbury	1936		
27¼	Stanford-Le-Hope	1854		
32¼	Pitsea	1855		
Direct Southend line				
9½	Becontree	6/1926		Originally 'Gale Street halt'
11¼	Dagenham	5/1885		LT station originally 'Heathway'
13¾	Hornchurch	5/1885	LT stations	
15¼	Upminster	5/1885	from 9/1932	
19¼	West Horndon	5/1886		Originally 'East Horndon'
22¾	Laindon	1888		
24½	Basildon	11/1974		Date for second station
26½	Pitsea	6/1888		
29¼	Benfleet (for Canvey Island)	7/1855		Rebuilt and resited 8/1921
32½	Leigh-on-Sea	7/1855		Rebuilt and resited 4/1934
34	Chalkwell	9/1933		
34¾	Westcliff	1895		Originally 'on Sea'
35¾	Southend Central	1856		Originally 'on Sea'
36¾	Southend East	7/1932		
38	Thorpe Bay	7/1910		'Southchurch on Sea' for first 17 days
39½	Shoeburyness	2/1884		
Romford and Ockendon branches				
	Upminster			
1¾	Emerson Park	10/1909		Originally 'Halt'
3½	Romford	6/1893 (LT&S)		
3¼	Ockendon	7/1892		

LINES FROM FENCHURCH STREET

LONDON COMMUTER LINES

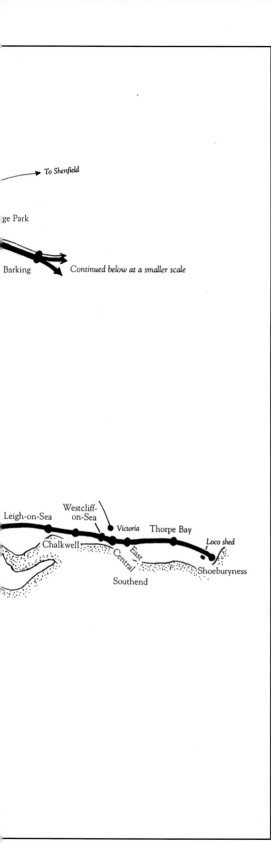

To Shenfield

ge Park

Barking — Continued below at a smaller scale

Leigh-on-Sea   Westcliff-on-Sea
Chalkwell   Victoria   Thorpe Bay
Central   East   Loco shed
Southend   Shoeburyness

distance traffic thereafter, reaching Barking in April 1908. In that year track quadrupling was completed between Bromley and Barking and extended to Upminster in September 1932, when District Line trains made it their outer terminus.

Fenchurch Street, then with five platforms, handled some 300 trains daily in 1930, and was rebuilt between 1932 and 1935 with two island platforms, the longer for LMS and the shorter for LNER trains. Services operated by the latter and its Eastern Region successor were either discontinued or transferred to Liverpool Street during the 1940s, leaving the LT&S trains as sole occupants at last. The station was further rebuilt commencing in December 1983 when the concourse was enlarged, but remains the only London terminus without direct access to the Underground; Tower Hill (Circle Line) and Tower Gateway (Docklands Light Railway) stations are both nearby.

Notwithstanding the generally flat terrain of Essex, the Southend direct line is by no means free from gradients, being generally downhill out to Plaistow. There is a slight hump at Upminster and a more pronounced one at Laindon, approached by gradients of 1 in 110 from either side. A third summit with similar grades is at Southend Central, so in steam days the locomotives had no easy task with their heavy peak-hour loads.

Limehouse station (formerly Stepney East), on a sharp curve just 1¾ miles from the terminus, and with a DLR station alongside, is now the only stop west of Barking, but accounts for only 0.1 per cent of LT&S section revenue. There was once a triangular junction here with the old L&B line to Blackwall and North Greenwich, closed in 1926. The four stations thence to Barking now retain platforms for the District Line tracks only, but 'LT&SR' monograms in the ironwork proclaim the original ownership at several of them. These stations were finally transferred from BR to London Transport Executive control in 1970.

Barking station was comprehensively rebuilt (for the second time) in 1959-62, with three island platforms for six through tracks and two terminal platforms, one each for District and Gospel Oak line trains. Track rearrangements

Left The exit from Fenchurch Street on 22 May 1991, as seen from the adjacent Docklands Light Railway station at Tower Gateway. EMU No 310060, built at Derby in 1965, is leaving for Southend via Upminster. *F. Hornby*

Middle left This is Limehouse, the first station out of Fenchurch Street, better known for many years as Stepney East. The sharply curved platforms, built on a viaduct, are seen in this view looking west on 9 March 1993. *F. Hornby*

Below The true spirit of the 'Tilbury' is captured in this scene at Barking on 11 October 1958. Stanier three-cylinder 2-6-4T No 42516 heads an eight-coach Shoeburyness train, with a District Line 'Metadyne' train in the background. The speed restriction sign on the left is in connection with construction of the flyover just beyond the bridge. *F. Hornby*

LONDON COMMUTER LINES

included a dive-under east of the station and a flyover at the west end, facilitating cross-platform interchange between westbound trains on the District and LT&S lines, together with a second flyover for freights between Ripple Lane yards and Woodgrange Park. The station buildings, spanning the tracks at right-angles, are of an impressive modernistic design with a spacious hall incorporating booking offices and shops.

As mentioned in Chapter 5, some steam trains via the Tottenham & Forest Gate line used to terminate at a bay platform at East Ham until 1958, after which the spur from Woodgrange Park was subsequently removed. The main LT&S depot for electric units is between the up and down lines just east of East Ham, on a site previously occupied by a London Transport depot.

Immediately beyond Barking the Tilbury and Southend routes part company, the latter continuing more or less due east, accompanied on the north side by the District Line tracks, along which five new stations were provided in the 1930s. One main reason for the extension

was the building of the LCC Becontree Estate, now with 90,000 residents, adjoining the populous Hornchurch Urban District with Upminster at its eastern extremity. The station here is important, being the first stop east of Barking for LT&S trains, and the junction for the single-track lines north to Romford and south to Grays, as well as being the District Line terminus. There are four through platforms – those for the District Line giving access to the depot east of the station – with terminal platforms for each of the branches.

The Romford-Upminster line opened in 1893, one year after the Upminster-Grays section, and had one intermediate station. Both lines are worked by self-contained shuttle services.

Continuing eastward, the modern town of Basildon, with 150,000 inhabitants, ranks fifth in revenue importance on the LT&S section, although the BR authorities were slow to recognise the need for a station there; one was eventually opened in November 1974. Next comes Pitsea, the junction with the eastern end of the Tilbury loop, and thereafter the railway is in close proximity to the Thames Estuary,

Judging by appearances the LT&S platforms on the right at Becontree are little used, as seen in this view looking east on 12 May 1961. Although the catenary is in place, all services were still steam worked at that point. Even the District Line platforms are devoid of life at what must be an 'off-peak' hour! B. W. L. Brooksbank

Time was when these platforms would have been crowded with day trippers to 'Sarfend'! The scene at Southend Central on 19 October 1993 is far more tranquil, with a Class 302 EMU in the terminal platform on a service to Fenchurch Street via Tilbury. *F. Hornby*

serving a succession of resort-cum-residential towns of which Southend itself (pop 156,000) is the largest. Gone are the days when the 'Kursaal' amusement park, the cockle-and-whelk stalls and the mile-long pier (with its own railway) drew vast crowds of daytrippers – your author went there from East Putney on the District Line as a small boy in 1937!

Nowadays most of the revenue is derived from commuters and shoppers, though surprisingly Southend comes no higher than tenth in the revenue chart. The Central station has two terminal platforms facing London as well as the two through lines which continue for a further 3¾ miles to Shoeburyness. The station there is simple, with wooden buildings, but there are extensive stabling sidings for electric multiple units. All traces of the four-road steam shed have disappeared.

The Tilbury loop is of a very different nature,

at least for the first 14 miles, past what remains of Ripple Lane yards and the environs of Dagenham, with the huge rail-connected Ford Motor Works to the south of the line and the town to the north. After Rainham and Purfleet the branch from Upminster comes in at West Thurrock Junction, three-quarters of a mile short of Grays station.

Tilbury Town, hard by the container port, is unimpressive with its two through platforms, by contrast with the Riverside terminus, which closed in November 1992. Connected to the loop line by a triangle junction, it had six platform faces and dealt with boat trains from St Pancras until 1963 as well as the Fenchurch Street and Southend services; nowadays rail passengers for the adjacent Tilbury-Gravesend ferry must use a bus connection from the Town station. In steam days a busy motive power depot occupied a site within the triangle.

The once-bustling Tilbury Riverside station looks forlorn and deserted in this February 1986 scene, with EMU No 308152 about to depart for Upminster. The buildings once contained a customs hall and all the amenities required for passengers on cruise ships and the regular Swedish Lloyd sailings. *F. Hornby*

This BR Class '4P' 2-6-4T, recorded at Benfleet on 12 May 1961, has only a few months more of active service ahead on the Tilbury section, as witness the catenary already in position. The station, 29¼ miles from London, opened in July 1855. *B. W. Brooksbank*

The Tilbury-Pitsea section dates from 1846 and skirts sand and gravel pits before passing to the west of Stanford-le-Hope town, 5 miles short of the junction at Pitsea. The maximum permissible speed throughout the Tilbury loop is 60 mph, as compared with 75 mph on favourable sections of the main line via Upminster.

Electrification first came to Fenchurch Street in 1949 when it was intended to run a 1,500V DC shuttle service to and from Stratford via Bow Junction. The scheme proved abortive, but the connection came into its own in February 1953 when the LT&S line was flooded east of Benfleet and a service between the Great Eastern section and Fenchurch Street was organised for the benefit of Southend passengers. It also proved useful, after conversion to 6.25kV AC current, for transferring stock between the two sections. This was after electrification of LT&S lines in 1961-62, when two different voltages were adopted for clearance reasons. The power supply out of Fenchurch Street was at 6.25kV AC to points about half a mile beyond Barking on both lines, and eastwards from just beyond Leigh-on-Sea. The intermediate mileage, including the Upminster-Grays line, was at 25kV AC. The Romford-Upminster line was excluded and did not find itself 'under the wires' for another 25 years, but by mid-1989 the higher voltage had been standardised throughout the LT&S section.

Resignalling in preparation for the new traction was completed in August 1961, extending colour-lights and track circuiting along the whole of the Shoeburyness main line and the Tilbury loop. The freight-only Thames Haven branch retained absolute block working, and the electric token blocks on the Romford-Upminster line remained in use until colour-lights were installed in November 1978.

At Fenchurch Street, the 1935-built electro-mechanical box spanning the tracks outside the station originally had 140 levers controlling four-aspect colour-lights at the platforms and approaches. In 1961 a push-button panel was installed, for remote control of Stepney East and Gas Factory Junctions, and after track rationalising the number of levers was reduced to 33.

On the direct route via Upminster 41 signal boxes were replaced by nine, including new power-operated installations at Barking, Pitsea and Southend Central. On the Tilbury loop 21 boxes were reduced to 12, with a new power cabin opened at Tilbury. The new installations permitted 2-minute headways along the direct route, while at the same time a start was made to replace the Hudd system of Automatic Train Control dating from 1947 with the BR standard Automatic Warning System. Another innovation, then unique on BR, was the provision of electric train description apparatus in 12 signal boxes, automatically linked to a control office at Fenchurch Street.

The 3½-mile Romford-Upminster line was electrified at 25kV AC during 1985/86 at a cost of £303,000, and free rides were given when the first electric trains ran on 12 May 1986. The terminal platform at Romford was duly lengthened to accommodate a four-coach unit.

Looking to the future, under a new resignalling project it is intended to replace all 17 remaining signal boxes, including that at Fenchurch Street, by a new centre at Upminster, in conjunction with track alterations to permit reversible running on all lines.

Services

In the Summer 1948 timetable there were 74 departures from Fenchurch Street on weekdays, of which 47 were routed via Upminster and 27 via the Tilbury loop. Forty of the former and seven of the latter were through trains to Shoeburyness, involving of course a reversal at Riverside station for those via Tilbury. Six terminated at Riverside and 14 continued to Pitsea, Southend or Thorpe Bay. On Saturdays the half-day was catered for by no fewer then 23 departures between 11.25 am and 2.00 pm. Even on Sundays the departure total stood at a respectable 44, though one could well visualise how peaceful it would be at Fenchurch Street on the Sabbath!

Although hard work with heavy loads and smart running was required, overall average speeds fell mostly within the range of 20-38 mph, as demonstrated by the examples in the table below.

The Romford-Upminster-Grays link saw 22 trains each way between Romford and Upminster, plus three continuing to Grays and one through to Tilbury. There were ten from Upminster to Tilbury and three from Grays to Tilbury, plus two return trips between Upminster and Ockendon. On Sundays six trains ran through each way between Tilbury and Romford, allowed between 49 and 66 minutes for the 14¼ miles.

The following year (1949) saw the introduction of regular-interval services on both the main line and Tilbury loop, which were adhered to with minor changes until electrification. Off peak there were hourly fast and slow trains via Upminster to Southend and beyond, and one to Southend via Tilbury, with variations of intermediate stops. The slow trains to Shoeburyness via Upminster took 92 minutes (25.75 mph), but the fast trains made some smart running, with the palm going to the 4 pm from Fenchurch Street, non-stop to Westcliff in 44 minutes (47.5 mph). At rush hours and at Bank Holiday weekends some Tilbury trains started or terminated at Barking, while one early morning up train from Pitsea via Tilbury avoided Riverside, running direct via the north curve.

When electric working commenced in late 1961 it was not at first possible to implement the full service, thanks to the temporary retention of some units on the GE section. Once the full fleet was available the weekday departures from Fenchurch Street totalled 134 – an 80 per cent increase over 1948. Six trains left hourly off-peak, four for Shoeburyness via Upminster and two via Tilbury. Faster trains at peak hours produced times such as 37 minutes to Leigh-on-Sea with one stop (52.75 mph). However, as is often the case, some 'pruning' took place in due course; from 7 November 1966 the service via Upminster was reduced to three per hour with additional stops, though a

Example journeys on LT&S lines, 1948

Journey	Distance (miles)	Stops	Time (min)	Average (mph)
Fenchurch St-Shoeburyness (via Upminster)	39½	19	111	21.35
Fenchurch St-Shoeburyness (via Upminster)	39½	10	84	27.5
Fenchurch St-Southend (via Upminster)	35¾	6	56	37.3
Fenchurch St-Shoeburyness (via Tilbury Riverside)	45¼	23	133	20.41
Fenchurch St-Tilbury Riverside	22½	10	71	19.0
Fenchurch St-Tilbury Riverside	22½	8	56	24.1

With numerous 1960-vintage units still in service, one wonders why a comparatively modern 90 mph Class 312 has been diagrammed for the 3-mile trip from Upminster to Ockendon! Possibly it is on a 'running in' turn after a visit to the works for the EMU's equivalent of a '10,000-mile service'! *F. Hornby*

few weeks later one train hourly was speeded up again. Nevertheless, patronage was up by 60 per cent in 1968 as compared with 1959, with over 67,000 passengers using Fenchurch Street every weekday.

In 1970 there was a spate of cancellations due to staff shortages and equipment failures, but in the May timetable for that year improvements were made in the services to the Estuary towns, with some trains terminating short of Southend Central. Again, in May 1973, the 'regular-interval' principle was applied to peak hours, so that in the down direction six trains left Fenchurch Street in each of four consecutive 15-minute periods, giving fast services to a variety of stations.

Present-day frequencies fall slightly short of those in the first heady days of full electrification, with 117 weekday departures from Fenchurch Street in the 1993/94 timetable, plus three in the small hours of Mondays only. There are five hourly off-peak departures from Fenchurch Street, of which two serve the Tilbury loop, terminating at Southend Central, while the three via Upminster all go through to Shoeburyness. The fastest time to Leigh-on-Sea is 39 minutes with two stops, the corresponding up train being 3 minutes slower. Late at night four trains out of Liverpool Street serve LT&S destinations, via Forest Gate Junction and Barking.

The Romford-Upminster line has a half-hourly service – first introduced when diesel units took over in 1956 – while the longer section thence to Grays has to be content with an hourly through train, plus another shuttling between Upminster and Ockendon.

Traction and trains

In 1948 the LT&S section was 100 per cent steam operated, with depots at Plaistow (13A), Tilbury (13C), Shoeburyness (13D) and Upminster (13E), which, after transfer to the Eastern Region in 1949, became 33A, B and C, Upminster being relegated to sub-shed status. The combined allocation was around 140 locomotives, of which the majority were passenger tanks of the 2-6-4 and 4-4-2 types. The prime movers were Stanier's '4P' three-cylinder 2-6-4Ts Nos 42500-36, built in 1934 and humorously dubbed 'Tugboat Annies' thanks to their ship's-siren-style hooters. Most were based at Shoeburyness, with the remainder at Plaistow. There were also 25 Fowler, Stanier and Fairburn two-cylinder variants of the same wheel arrangement at Plaistow and Tilbury. They were supported by 39 '3P' 4-4-2Ts of LT&S design, some of them Derby-built as recently as 1930. Others of the class dated back to the late 1890s but had been substantially rebuilt, while a few surviving '2P' 4-4-2Ts of 1900 construction still languished at Plaistow or nearby Devons Road.

The '3Ps' did useful secondary work, particularly on the Tilbury loop, including those trains that, at busy weekends, started or terminated at Barking. Many were withdrawn

Above In this busy scene at Tilbury on 2 April 1960 Class '4P' 2-6-4T No 42511 heads a stopping train of Eastern Region stock from Fenchurch Street to Riverside station. Among the locomotives in the shed yard, a 'WD' '8F' 2-8-0 and a Class '4' Ivatt 'Mogul' are visible. *F. Hornby*

Left In April 1951 ex-MR Johnson '1P' 0-4-4T No 58045 stands alongside the wooden terminal platform at Romford prior to departure for Upminster. At this juncture the 1884-built locomotive has a life expectancy of barely seven months. The GE section Colchester main line is in the background. *F. Hornby*

Left A train of Class AM2 units in green livery with No 246 leading arrives at Barking on 11 April 1964 en route to Shoeburyness. The District Line track climbing steeply on to the flyover can just be glimpsed on the extreme left. *F. Hornby* or dispersed further afield when displaced by 28 BR Standard Class '4' 2-6-4Ts, newly built from 1953-56. By this time the Fowler engines had left the section and the assorted fleet of some 81 ex-LMS and BR 2-6-4Ts held the fort until electrification. After the Eastern Region took control a proposal to draft in 'L1' 2-6-4Ts was considered and rejected, possibly because of the expense of fitting ATC gear. One wonders how they would have coped with 13-coach trains grossing 350 tons over a difficult road?

During the summer there were numerous through workings off the Midland and Western Divisions of the LMR, for which purpose 4-6-0s, 2-6-0s and 0-6-0s from the London sheds were fitted with the ATC apparatus.

The small shed at Upminster maintained five ex-MR '1P' 0-4-4Ts equipped for push-pull working on the lines to Romford and Grays, including one of 1876 vintage that was withdrawn in 1954. However, the '3P' 4-4-2Ts were no strangers to these lines in earlier years, as for example in November 1949 when the author travelled behind one in a six-coach train from Tilbury Riverside to Upminster. On the demise of the 0-4-4Ts their replacements were auto-fitted 'N7' 0-6-2Ts from Stratford shed, one of which made the last steam-hauled run before DMUs took over on 17 September 1956. The Grays line remained the preserve of steam traction until January 1958, with a short appearance thereon by ex-GNR 'C12' 4-4-2Ts and by a pair of '3F' 'Jinty' 0-6-0Ts, a menial duty shared at times by non-auto-fitted 2-6-4Ts.

Plaistow shed closed in June 1962 and in the same month Tilbury lost its passenger engines and became a 'sub' to Stratford for freight work only. One of the last steam workings was a down rush-hour train on 15 June of that year hauled by No 42501, which, by coincidence, was the last engine to leave Shoeburyness for scrapping. The footplate staff retrained as motormen, working from the new depot at East Ham, while their former steeds were dumped at Plaistow and Shoeburyness, where both shed buildings were eventually demolished.

Steam-hauled coaching stock included ex-LT&SR, MR, LMS, LNER and eventually BR

standard vehicles. At nationalisation there were 17 sets of 11 close-coupled 54-foot carriages of LMS origin, each including two lavatory composites, of 1924-34 construction. Ex-MR set trains were made up of elliptical-roofed 48-foot and 50-foot carriages with both Westinghouse and vacuum brakes, while ex-LT&SR vehicles, mostly eight-compartment 3rds, survived until 1956.

The first post-war additions comprised six four-coach sets with bodies of early Eastern Region design mounted on ex-GER 54-foot frames; some had centre gangways and toilets. There were also 30 coaches of post-war LNER suburban design, replacing ex-MR 13-coach rakes, and from 1954 onwards four variations of BR standard vehicles appeared. Latterly more ER and BR stock arrived, formed into 8- and 11-coach trains, releasing early LMS wooden-bodied coaches for scrapping. Thus by the late 1950s many trains consisted of ex-LNER/ER stock, hauled by ex-LMS engines!

The first electric multiple units were four-car sets of Class AM2 (later 302), of which 112 were built for the LT&S section by BR at Doncaster and York. After trials in June 1961 they took over some services on steam schedules in November. A full service was running by March 1962 after 24 units had returned from loan to the GE section. Some 30 units are still on LT&S duties in the 1990s after refurbishing with fluorescent lighting and a public address system.

For nearly 30 years, with some interchange between East Ham and Ilford (GE) depots, the LT&S fleet consisted entirely of EMUs of 1960 vintage, all dual voltage and of 'High Density' designs with slam-doors to each seating bay. Early on the scene were five sloping-fronted four-car Class AM8 (308/2) units, uniquely incorporating a Motor Luggage Van. These were rebuilt in 1971 and reclassified 308/4, with the MLVs converted to Motor Brake Seconds, and in 1984 were again modified as parcel units, now withdrawn. Also used on the stopping services have been Classes 305/1, 305/2 and 308/1; the 1974 allocation at East Ham consisted of 96 units, reduced slightly by 1986 to 85 of Classes 302 and 308.

By the end of the 1980s the whole section

was taking current at 25kV AC, thus eliminating the need for units equipped for dual voltage, and it became possible to draft in 38 Class 310 four-coach sets, originally built in 1965 for outer-suburban services from Euston. With a better power-to-weight ratio than the 'High Density' designs and with bodies based on Mk II coaching stock, they are still currently responsible for many of the faster duties.

A crisis arose in 1991 when 35 units were taken out of service after overheating of cooling oil in transformers had started fires. As a precautionary measure all motor coaches were locked until the faults were rectified, drastically reducing seating capacity. Fortunately, by this time 17 of the 90 mph Class 312s of 1976 design were on LT&S metals and were not similarly affected.

In October 1993 the Class 308 units, by now refurbished, were transferred away, leaving Classes 302, 310 and 312 to cover all duties, the peak-hour requirement being for 80 units with maximum 12-coach formations. Additionally, Ilford-based Class 315 three-car suburban units work the Romford-Upminster service.

Thanks to the transition directly from steam to electric traction, diesels have played only a minor role in the LT&S section story. In early BR years the less than successful experimental Bo-Bo locomotive No 10800 ran trials for a few months, and in 1958 an ML2 Bo-Bo of the D61XX series equally failed to distinguish itself on Barking-Tilbury duties. More successful were the Brush Type 2 A1A-A1A D55XX machines, which filled in on passenger work at weekends when released from freight traffic.

Diesel multiple units have largely been confined to the Romford-Upminster-Grays routes; Derby twin units took over from the 'N7s' between Romford and Upminster in September 1956, and appeared on the Upminster-Grays line from January 1958. They were ultimately replaced by Craven Class 105s, which remained on the former line until electrification in 1986. For a time from the end of 1958 diesel units also worked a shuttle service between Tilbury and Pitsea, connecting with steam-hauled trains at either end.

Although there have been rumours of Class 321 units being drafted to the LT&S section, none has yet appeared at the time of writing, so for the immediate future the 310s, 312s and even the remaining 302s look set fair to continue to shoulder the burden!

INDEX